LIGHT,

at the End of the Bench

CJ

First paperback edition, August 2023

ISBN 979-8-9887590-0-3

Back cover image: Sofia Marie Coronado

Book design by Nuno Moreira, NM DESIGN

LIGHT,

at the End of the Bench

NIKSHA
FEDERICO

To my Mom,
Without you, I am nothing. I love you.

PRAISE FOR LIGHT, AT THE END OF THE BENCH

"Federico vividly illustrates the walk-on experience. His words trace the emotional arc of my own journey, and he deftly captures the humbling, yet inspiring, nature of being a walk-on.

As a walk-on, you start in last place, and overcoming that entry point was incredibly challenging and rewarding. I had to surrender my ego and work harder than ever before. Finding my way was an exercise in optimism and determination. Luckily, I was able to learn that lesson while building lifelong friendships. Similar to the story of this book, my experience helped me establish a roadmap for success and emboldened me to bet on myself. Federico's tale will inspire many, and it was a joy reading about his ride."

> - Robbie Lemons, Sacramento Kings Senior Director, Coaching Analytics & Strategy

"Niksha Federico has shown all of us how much we can get and give, when we walk-on any court of any kind in life."

> - David Hollander, Professor NYU, author How Basketball Can Save the World

"In LIGHT, AT THE END OF THE BENCH Federico leaves it all out there. The book is his basketball court, and within its boundaries, we feel the emotional highs and lows, the internal and external runs, the momentum shifts. Somehow, someway he has to make it. He chose to do something so unique and everlasting with his experiences—he leaned into fears, pressed into pressures, and discovered something much bigger than playing time: A life-time."

- Dr. Oliver Eslinger, Head Basketball Coach Caltech, Performance Psychology, NeuroPerformance, Neuroscience, NABC Guardian of the Game

"A deep story from the heart. Debut author Niksha Federico instantly plants himself into the non-fiction space with his inspiring, yet practical, story, "Light, at the End of the Bench." As a former walk-on myself, I found a striking amount of similarities between our journeys. This book does a tremendous job of illustrating both the highs, and lows that accompany elite level athletics. I loved every page of this book and know it will touch the lives of a variety of readers around the globe."

- JD Slajchert, motivational speaker, philanthropist, author of MoonFlower, and Darling, You're Not Alone

"Starting my career at a world class organization and navigating the corporate pressure cooker could have been easier had I read Niksha's incredible book and taken it to heart early in my time climbing the corporate ladder from the bottom rung."

- John Lohrenz, President JKL Wealth Management, author of The Prosperity Project, Former U.S. Merrill Lynch Manager of the Year

"I wasn't a walk-on, but I definitely was an underdog. The actual take away is that you really have a choice. A choice of how to react, how to make the most of whatever the situation is. Light, at the End of the Bench hit home for me, and I highly recommend this book for any athlete trying to find an edge."

- Lindsey Napela Berg, 3x Olympian, 2x Silver Medalist, Former USA Volleyball Athlete of the Year

"A true story of perseverance and belief that illustrates the challenges and decisions that come with being a "walk on". Being Niksha's roommate, as well as teammate for a year of professional basketball in Spain, it became clear to me how he navigated being a 4 year walk-on, to finding the tremendous success he has. His daily habits, mindset, and constant reflection allowed him to make "the grind" look effortless. This book gives the blueprint of how he did it, and tells the story in a raw, honest, and conversational way. We all start as a "walk on" at some point, regardless of what job you have or where you are in your life, a time will come when you are the small fish. This book gives real stories of the highs and the lows and will encourage you to take that leap of faith."

- Kimbal Mackenzie, Professional Basketball Player, Great-Britain National Team, Leicester Riders, Former 4x Captain Bucknell University Men's Basketball, Former Patriot League Student-Athlete of the Year

"A story of real patience and determination. From being an anonymous walk-on in college, to a successful professional basketball player. LIGHT, AT THE END OF THE BENCH is a true example of the amount of hard work and sacrifice it takes to make leaps in levels, the highs and lows of betting on yourself, and the importance of believing in your vision. I was honored to be his Head Coach as a professional in Spain.

Since my first conversation with him on the phone I knew I wanted him to be a part of my program. I felt he had been through a lot in basketball, which had only built the strength of his grit and character as a player. His mindset took us to another level and pushed us forward to win a Championship. This book is personal, while uniquely portraying the high-level awareness + basketball IQ Niksha holds both on and off the court. Grab a few espressos and get ready to embark on an inspirational journey."

> - Hugo Lopez, Professional Basketball Head Coach, Former Sweden Men's National Team Head Coach, Former Real Valladolid Head Coach & Real Madrid Basketball

"LIGHT, AT THE END OF THE BENCH could not have been anything less than a perfect title for Niksha's debut book. As he goes in depth about his experience as a walk-on, at a major basketball school; he vividly paints the picture of what it's like to persevere when all the odds are against you. Playing with Federico for a year in Spain and becoming close friends with him over the years, it's easy to see how and why he's been successful in life. His story is proof that it's not about where you start, but rather how hard you work and trust in your vision. I believe this book will have an incredible impact on readers around the world."

> - Frank Bartley IV, Professional Basketball Player, Pallacanestro Trieste,

Former Brigham Young & University of Louisiana - Lafayette Men's Basketball, Former Sunbelt Conference Newcomer of the Year, Former Southern District Mid Major Player of the Year, 2020 Eurobasket Import of the Year

"This story is captivating beyond measure from beginning to end. The growth of Federico is truly on display to all readers throughout the book, his mental edge is unnerving, multi-faceted in multiple ventures, and he is never afraid to break through the boundaries placed around him.

Having a unique perspective of spending a year with him in Spain, I witnessed first-hand how he operates, learning a lifetime of lessons in a short period. The 10 min cold showers, countless hours of reading book after book, daily meditation, while having a relentless determination to improve his basketball skills on court. Light, at the End of the Bench reiterates to an entire generation, that hard work is paramount in all aspects of life and that if seeds are planted early, with constant nurture and attention, then trees will eventually blossom. That is the substance Niksha exemplifies and looks to build up on as he continues his young illustrious career."

- Kingsley Okoroh, Professional Basketball Player, University of California Berkeley

"Niksha's walk-on experience/mentality provides an array of tips and mental frameworks which systematically shifts the paradigm of what it means to be a walk-on. The emotional awareness and maturity displayed in this book will radically strengthen the mindset for not only future walk-ons, but everyday underdogs as well."

- D.B. Williams, serial-entrepreneur, strategic advisor, philanthropist

"We don't live the same stories, but we all suffer the same way."

— Margot Sebban

"Genius is perseverance in disguise."
— Mike Newlin

CONTENTS

Walk-on: "An unrecruited athlete who becomes part of a team without promised opportunity or financial incentive."

"An unknown intern who gets a job at a company without having any connections."

"A young artist moving away from a small town to a big city."

"A first-generation medical student attempting to become a doctor."

"A former professional athlete transitioning from sports to starting fresh as a creative writer."

Each one of us faces the transitional challenges of being a "walk-on".

FOREWORD

I met Niksha in August of 2019 when he arrived in Valladolid, Spain. A tall lanky young man with a deep baritone voice who kept answering me with "Yes Sirs" and "No Sirs". We had done our scouting and research on him, and he represented to the core everything our young basketball club was all about. First, let me explain to you the beginnings of our professional club.

Back in the summer of 2015, Valladolid's historic basketball club folded after years of turmoil and toying constantly with bankruptcy. I had played for the club back in the early nineties. The club had an amazing pedigree of great players, the likes of Arvydas Sabonis, Oscar Schmidt, Carlton Myers, "Hot Plate" Williams and the list goes on. When the club finally declared itself insolvent, I decided to start a new club from scratch, or better said from the six-feet deep.

My father once told me that if I were ever in the position to give back to basketball everything it had given me, to do so, because it would be a tremendous satisfaction. My leadership skills would play a big part in carrying out this huge challenge. No one was brave enough, nor crazy enough to take the first step, in fact many of my friends told me not to do it; that I would fail and ruin my good reputation. Well, I have never been one to back away from a challenge or avoid taking the last second shot. Being afraid to fail is basically failure all in itself. The biggest challenge was to regain credibility. Years of debts, unpaid salaries, and broken promises had taken its toll on a blue-collar city that finally turned its back on the club. How would I tackle this beast? Leading by example, endless hours of hard work, many sleepless nights, economic responsibility, getting the city and province involved, giving the local players a chance to be on the team, recruiting hungry and hardnosed players, and sticking to our philosophy from day one until the end no matter how much success or failure we endured. Leaders must understand what is best for the collective and have to be willing to take unfair shots and criticism from the press and from many people you don't expect. You are the shield for everyone, and you must do all the dirty work so no one can hold anything against you. I was a sports director, a custodian, a PR man, a mover, a taxi driver, a marketing man, an accountant, I pretty much covered all the fields you can imagine inside a club while being president. That is why people started following us and believing in us again. I remember a friend of mine telling me "Mike, you are the president, you can't be on your knees unpeeling the publicity stickers from the floor after the games. It's a bad image for the club." I told him that to unclog the toilet drain, you got to be willing to get your hands dirty!

I firmly believe that Niksha and I possess very similar

leadership qualities, in my case obtained by years of experience in the game of life, and in his through patience, grit, and learning to embrace the discomfort that being a walk-on creates. He weathered many a storm, learning leadership the hard way. Both of us have been doubted, ruled out, told we couldn't achieve our dream; but here we are today, fulfilled leaders looking for new challenges in life.

It didn't take long for Niksha to win us over with his work ethic, demeanor, mentality, and relentless effort on both ends of the court on every single possession. Niksha was the player all championship teams need. He was our glue, the player who did all the dirty work, analyzing every game and going to work like a neurosurgeon with pinpoint precision at his craft.

If he had to lock-up the opponent's top scorer, it was done. If we needed him to crash the glass, he was the best in the league. If we needed scoring, he could drop twenty-five in a heartbeat. If hustle points showed up on the stat sheets, he would have won the category in a landslide.

It is very uncharacteristic to see a young American player in his second professional season overseas be so unselfish and sacrifice himself and his numbers for the betterment of the team. At the very core that is who Niksha is, a multi-faceted natural born leader, comprised of seamless winning character. Character molded from years of being at the end of the bench. It was beautiful to watch his ability to read each situation and give the team exactly what was needed of him at that given moment of the game. I have played and seen a lot of basketball in my career, and I knew we had something special from the first day of training camp.

I could never have imagined that we were going to be the last team Niksha played for. That season we were in first place, commanding the standings from week three all the way to the end. We were the talk of the league for our up-tempo and unselfish style of basketball, going undefeated at home. We upset all the teams that were supposed to be better than us, and in the midst of preparing to celebrate a championship for the entire city we ran into a rival that would devastate and cause so much pain and anguish to so many people around the world; Covid-19.

I was puzzled at first when I heard Niksha was taking the year off, but it wouldn't be until after I read this book and talked to him that I finally understood everything.

When is it time to turn the page and start a new challenge in life? When is it time to apply the discipline and mentality learned as a high-level athlete, to the next phase?

That is a very difficult and challenging moment in the career of an athlete, but Niksha didn't budge a second. I applaud, respect, and admire his bold decision. The sacrifice, discipline, anxiety, and his share of sleepless nights just to have a slight edge for that last roster spot, made him see and appreciate basketball from a totally different perspective. His keen foresight told him it was time to get going onto his next endeavor. Those years at the end of the bench, built a natural leader, ready to delay gratification and embrace adversity head on.

In an analytic driven world, you can't quantify leadership, you can't quantify fearlessness, you can't quantify HEART, but in *Light, at the End of the Bench* Niksha has demonstrated that starting out as a walk-on could be a new form of quantification for the characteristics needed to thrive in this ever-changing transformative world. It has been a long time coming and only someone like Niksha could pull it off. I strongly recommend this book, not only for your die-hard basketball fan, but for all those who appreciate hard work, passion, resilience, out of the box thinking, and perseverance.

The great John Wooden once said "Players with fight never lose a game, they just run out of time." Well, that defines Niksha to perfection on the court. Off the court, he will be successful at anything he sets his mind to. This book is just as small sample size of everything he has in store for us.

Just wait and see!

Mike Hansen – Former President CBC Valladolid Basketball Club

INTRODUCTION

"The greatest task we have in life is to share the knowledge and skills
we accumulate. It doesn't have to be more complex than that."
— Naval Ravikant

I might be a basketball player, but basketball is simply a
vehicle for the bigger story here...

Most people see someone's success without truly
understanding the trials and tribulations that person faced
to get to where they are. Let's be real: Starting out as a walk-
on means you are at the bottom rung of a long ladder—and
everybody knows it. This book is not only for current walk-
ons but for anybody who is starting somewhere new and has
a large hill to climb. My goal is to highlight a person's ability
to thrive at the bottom, build confidence, and persevere.

The walk-on mentality can be found in anyone. The
beauty of a walk-on story is that we are all walk-ons at
some point in our lives. No matter our personality, age, or
profession, we have all found ourselves in an unfamiliar
setting at the bottom of the ladder.

I began this book just a year out of college, sitting in
my apartment in Spain and reflecting on what it had taken
to secure a professional basketball contract. I looked back at

everything I had experienced along my path from unknown four-year walk-on to becoming one of the top players in the Spanish professional leagues. That journey involved flipping the script and turning my setbacks into fuel for success.

What's funny is, I remembered that, in the beginning, becoming a walk-on didn't sound too difficult. I would showcase my talents at an open tryout, and, if fortunate enough to make the team, I would reap the benefits of being a DI athlete: priority registration for classes, cool gear, a jersey with my name on the back, etc. I thought I had it figured out based on what was available at the time. I soon realized I had no idea what being a walk-on entailed or what it would require of me for four years of my life.

"Being considered a walk-on is far more common in college sports than most families and athletes realize. According to the latest NCAA information, 46 percent of DI athletes are walk-ons, and 39 percent of DII athletes are walk-ons. DIII athletes are not eligible to receive athletic scholarships, so walk-on status is not calculated." (5) (USA TODAY HS-S)

After speaking with several current and former walk-ons across the country, I noticed similar patterns. I realized this huge group of hopeful athletes lacked important information on the challenges of becoming a walk-on. They had no resources, guides, or community to help them. The thought of others having to go in blind—as I did—seemed wrong to me, and that compelled me to write this book. I know that my story, and the perspectives I have gained, can provide valuable information to help walk-ons in any field.

My journey was full of real challenges that go far beyond basketball. I dealt with depression and performance anxiety, which I had never encountered as a high school basketball standout. The game I loved turned into a nightmare. I felt trapped and questioned everything. I started to wonder if I was the only athlete going through this, if others were also struggling. I knew I couldn't be the only one.

Through my story, I will paint a picture of what being a walk-on is <u>actually</u> like. I'll tell you about the tactics I used, the outcomes I manifested, and the detail-oriented mentality I developed to build momentum and go from walk-on to professional.

Although the majority of this book focuses on success in sports, I want to reiterate that the definition of successful walk-on extends far beyond athletics. Everyone has their own reasons for becoming a walk-on at a university program, and many include goals other than playing time, getting a scholarship, or reaching the pros. Many athletes want to be a walk-on because they want to be part of something bigger than themselves. I simply wanted to experience what it was like to play collegiate sports at the highest level. It had been my dream since I was a little kid. Becoming a walk-on is about your own personal fulfillment. It's about being happy and trying to get the most out of your talents and hard work. A walk-on's experience varies from person to person. There is no right or wrong answer. The power to define what success truly looks like is in your hands.

So, if you're starting a new position, a new career, or just feeling down about a large hill you have to climb in life; if you want to grow or break free of the cage you have been put in; if you have ever felt like an underdog, have been overlooked, and want to use those experiences to your advantage—I hope this book helps you evolve your perspective and embrace your inner walk-on.

My entire soul is spread throughout the pages of this book; every word comes from the bottom of my heart. Whether you find the entire book helpful—or even a single chapter or quote—so long as you know you're not alone in your journey, the book will be a success in my eyes.

I want to congratulate you on making it this far. Welcome to *Light, at the End of the Bench*.

Sincerely,
Niksha Federico

59, 58, 57, 56 . . .

Down two.

Biggest game of the year.

Home court.

First place is on the line.

Bragging rights are on the line.

Our team's pride is on the line.

I tell myself, "BE READY." I need to be locked in if the ball comes to me.

My teammate secures the rebound, dribbles full-speed up the court, tries to get us an advantage.

Nothing there.

Every player understands how serious each possession is now. We all know we have to get the best shot possible.

My teammate slows the ball, dishes to our point guard.

From the far side, I notice our best scorer is matched up against our opponent's smaller point guard.

48, 47, 46 . . .

The entire crowd is on their feet, nervously watching as our top scorer gets closer to the basket.

45, 44, 43 . . .

My teammate prepares to shoot. The opposition runs to double team; he picks up his dribble. I see my defender cheating away from me. It's all the space I need. I wave my arm and lock eyes with my teammate.

42, 41, 40 . . .

All the chemistry we have built in practice pays off. He

throws a cross-court, over-his-shoulders bullet straight into my hands.

Time slows down. The entire arena gasps in unison. They know it's my shot for the taking.

I load up, ready to take the shot I have drained thousands of times in practice. Hours and hours. Thousands of shots.

In my peripheral vision, I see my defender realize he's messed up his assignment and given a shooter too much space.

I pump fake. My defender goes flying past me. I check my feet, toes behind the 3-point line, the rim out there waiting, 10,000 people now standing and staring in collective silence.

I glance at the shot clock: 4, 3, 2 . . .

I let it go, blacking out in the moment…SWISH!

The entire arena lets out a thunderous roar. I can't believe it. I'm numb. I pump my fist like Tiger Woods. My teammates swarm me, hugging and jumping on me.

Cameras converge all around me as I walk over to the bench, and Coach hugs me. His forehead sweaty, his eyes full of disbelief, he proudly says to me, "You've got some major balls, my friend!"

But my basketball journey wasn't always like this…

CHAPTER ONE

"Who you are is defined by what you're willing to struggle for."
— Mark Manson

From the first step, the walk-on route is a minefield of risk. You're either all-in or you're all-out. No lukewarm, no in-between. Yet, there's an element of beauty to this. Embracing this outlook can teach life lessons that apply to areas of life well beyond and much bigger than sport. However, it takes a mindset that understands the value of knowing you gave your everything for something meaningful, that understands the endless possibilities of that leap into the unknown.

Many are unable to envision the fulfillment beyond the horizon of risk or unprepared to take the first step beyond the borders of their comfort zones.

I know I was… Thankfully, my dad knew better.

* * *

To the best of their abilities, my parents had always supported me in everything I had ever wanted to do. But unfortunately, they weren't handed the secret blueprint to college basketball recruiting or privy to the accompanying hidden politics that sometimes surround them. So, like most of you, I blindly navigated the mysteries of athletics without a manual to follow...

I was blessed to be part of a great high school basketball team. We had the true characteristics of a winning team: elite team spatial recognition/cohesion, embedded altruistic culture, and not one selfish player. A perfect blend of egos led by a principle driven mentality that prioritized the "collective" over the "I".

Our class developed into one of the top teams in San Diego, winning the 2012 California Interscholastic Federation Championship (CIF) our junior year—the first for our school since 1998 & 2000, when Luke Walton (and brothers) had won us a banner. We entered our senior-year season ranked preseason No. 1 in San Diego County and convincingly won our league title. Unfortunately, we lost two games into our final state playoff run, which left a historic San Diego high school basketball team with ZERO DI prospects.

Personally, I had made huge strides between junior and senior year of high school—the definition of a late bloomer. I grew three inches during my senior year and got much stronger. Yet, when it came to recruiting, I had bloomed a few months too late. I finished my high school career as one of the best 3-point shooters in San Diego, which did attract some attention from DII and DIII schools, but no DI offers. Some prep schools on the East Coast were offering a year that would lead to guaranteed DI looks.

At the time, I decided neither option was right for me, that it was better to play it safe. So, I verbally committed to play at a smaller university. I liked the school—it offered a great education—and I was very comfortable being a big fish in a small pond. I was content, even excited.

A few days later, an acceptance letter arrived from San Diego State University (SDSU), and my father told me he had different plans: He had enrolled me, and I'd be attending orientation the next morning. I legitimately thought he was joking at first. I had already learned where I'd be living and picked my roommates! I knew where I wanted to be, and it was not at San Diego State. I was furious.

Fear causes a sense of inertia that keeps us from jumping into the unknown. I had never done anything that uncertain before. And it felt easy to stay where I was at, keep doing what I was doing. Tackling fear takes time. The first phase of battling fear is full-blown emotional discomfort, a shock to your senses.

From my dad's perspective, if I was serious about playing basketball, I needed to try to walk on at SDSU, where I could play for legendary head coach Steve Fisher. Dad believed in my talent, and that helped me believe in myself. He wanted me to take a leap of faith.

* * *

A collegiate walk-on is an athlete who gets neither a full athletic scholarship (DI, DII) nor any other financial incentive to attend a university (DIII), yet becomes part of a sports program in one of two ways: (1) as a preferred walk-on or (2) as an open-tryout walk-on. Preferred walk-ons have guaranteed spots so long as they are admitted by the school. Open tryout walk-ons get into school on academic merit and have to go through a one-day "audition" to impress the coaching staff. No guarantees. No safety nets. A single chance to make a first impression.

Each year, athletic programs across the nation host open tryouts to give regular students an opportunity to show off their skills and compete to make the team. Any full-time student can attend with the proper paperwork. Circumstances vary, but tryouts might last around two hours and could consist of up to 40–50 athletes fighting over one or two spots.

Of course, this is where things begin to get interesting. It doesn't matter how old you are, what you're studying, or where you're from. All that matters is how you perform on that one day. You play well, you make the team; if shots aren't falling, better luck next year. The odds are slim, but most serious athletes will love the opportunity. Welcome to the no-nonsense, job-oriented business of college sports!

For a potential walk-on, the deck is stacked somewhat against you. The gap between resources available to athletes with guaranteed spots and those available to walk-ons is always huge. At SDSU, for example, as a freshman I lived in the dorms like all normal students. Players on scholarship and preferred walk-ons were set up in apartments or houses upon arrival. Granted, housing and living situations vary between different programs and universities.

Also, until you are actually on the team, you have no access to the players' training facilities. So, what do you do? *Take initiative.* I found the Student Recreation Center on campus; it had basketball courts and a weight room, which was all I needed. The open tryout was in October, giving me two months to prepare. During that time, I focused on creating a disciplined routine: classes in the morning, then the library to study, and afterwards straight to the Rec for my daily workout, which was divided into three stages: weight training, shooting, and playing pick-up games. Consistency is key leading up to the tryout.

Knowing my skinny frame had likely played a role in the recruiting process, I made weight training a top priority. College basketball is a much different beast than high school. If you want to keep up, you need to focus consistently on improving in the weight room. The stronger you get, the better you'll be able to guard multiple positions. I began to be able to guard both forwards in the post and guards on the perimeter—something I wouldn't have been able to do without the additional strength training. The daily grind made my mind sharper as well. These improvements would play a crucial role on tryout day.

Anytime I'd think about the tryout, I'd have a weird mix of excitement and anxiety over how I'd match up against the other players I'd be competing against. So, every day, no matter what, I'd play pick-up games. It was a perfect way to stay in shape, and it gave me a way to evaluate the other guys who'd be competing for the same one or two spots. My thinking was, all the best student players who'd be trying out would eventually come play at the Rec. When I played there, I was playing differently than I would normally. I focused strictly on observing other players' tendencies— what worked for them, what didn't work. While they were playing to win, I was playing to LEARN in the moment so I could WIN on tryout day. The more I played with this perspective, the more aware I became. Programming my brain with this new perspective gave me a huge advantage during the tryout. I had learned not only the shooting or slashing ability of my competition, but I had picked up on all their emotional triggers.

However, with that date looming, all the amazing shots, dunks, and plays at the Rec meant nothing. Even though I had put in an extreme amount of work, I still felt a heavy weight on my shoulders. Regardless how much better I was getting, it would all boil down to performing in that two-hour window. The only reason I had enrolled at this school was for this opportunity. I had to deliver.

That's the reality of trying to make it as a walk-on.

You have to be able to perform under pressure. In a sense, it's really just the first test to see if you're built for all the challenges that the job (and life) entails.

I frequently get asked what open tryouts are like. Well, I can't sugarcoat this: It's a free-for-all. Many of the negative aspects involved in team sports come to life on tryout day: ball-hogging, selfishness, wild demeanor. Each player is hungry for a spot, dog eat dog. So be aware of that, and then put it behind you. Don't waste energy on negative factors beyond your control. Just direct your energy on what you can: attitude, confidence, extra effort, staying poised, etc.

"Control what you can control" might be one of the most overused sayings in athletics—as well as in life—but why do you think that is? Because it is powerful.

Find ways to identify unique competitive advantages in the months leading up to the tryout. For me, it was channeling open-mindedness and strategic creativity to build mental scouting reports on my competition.

Case in point: Head coaches rarely stay to watch an open tryout. Honestly, they are usually indifferent to who the walk-ons are. If the head coach does happen to be there, even better, but normally it will be an assistant coach running the show. That coach will then create a list of potential candidates to make the team. Given this responsibility, the assistant coach is looking for a player who can sustain playing at the level while also fitting the description of what is needed to help the team that year. Once the tryout is complete, the coordinating coach relays names back to the head coach and other members of the coaching staff. Then a decision is made—simple as that.

Now, the absence of the head coach doesn't change the fact that you're still being judged on every aspect of who you are throughout those two hours. Success on open-tryout day involves a lot more than just performing at a high level on the court. It means playing the right way, having great body language, and unshakeable demeanor. Don't complain when you get fouled. Don't yell at teammates for messing up. Small details play a big role in the overall assessment. I have seen far too many people direct their energy into the wrong channels—trying to get the most buckets, talking the most trash—when in reality that only hurts their chances of making the team. At the end of the day, college coaches will pass on an extremely talented player who has a negative attitude and an oversized ego. They don't want players who bring problems. They want players who have solid fundamentals, a desire to learn, and are willing to sacrifice their time to hustle, defend, rebound. Staying positive will only improve your chances of leaving a good impression and possibly securing a spot.

Luckily, when the day came, my theory was proven correct. When I showed up to the arena, almost every player at the tryout I had seen or played against at the Rec. My nervousness immediately transformed into confidence because I had mental scouting reports on each player. I knew I would have a serious chance of making the team if I performed well. That strategic advantage gave me a leg up and propelled my play to a higher level throughout that two-hour window. I could lock in and solely focus on myself during the drills.

TRYOUT DAY REGIMEN:
- Warmup: dribbling/ball-handling
- Layup lines
- Mid-range pull-ups
- 3-point shooting curls
- Fundamental/IQ drills
- Live competitive play (3-on-3, 4-on-4, 5-on-5)

I played well throughout, but when the tryout ended, I didn't know what to think. Like any audition or job interview, I left more focused on what I could have done better rather than what I had actually done well. After a couple days passed without receiving a call, I began to feel the anxiety creeping up on me, and definitely started overthinking things: *I guess I didn't make the team. Now what? What am I going to tell my friends? My dad? What the hell am I going to do?*

CHAPTER TWO

"Life shrinks or expands in proportion to one's courage."
— Anais Nin

I was checking my phone every two minutes for a notification. Blank. *Nothing.* A week and a half passed. While walking into the food hall for lunch, I received a call from an unknown number.

"Hey, Niksha." It was the team's player development coach, who would someday become a dear friend. "We would like to offer you a spot on the team. Congratulations. If you are still interested, come to practice tomorrow."

As calmly as I could, I said, "Yes, I am definitely still interested. Thank you so much. See you tomorrow."

I ended the call, then jumped into the air, threw up a vintage Tiger Woods fist pump, and screamed, "YES!" I was ecstatic. My leap of faith had come to fruition. I had officially accomplished my first and most important goal: I was on the team.

Now, if you're lucky enough to make the team through an open tryout, you need to understand the returning players on the team already have a three-month head start on you. The official team starts practicing and doing individual workouts during the first week of school. They have already had three months to build chemistry, improve dynamics, and solidify camaraderie for the new season. The first year you make the team, you are the odd one out. It takes time to become part of the culture. Accept this. Don't force it early on.

Arriving at Viejas Arena that first day, my head was spinning. I didn't know what to expect. I was nervous about meeting all my new teammates and coaches. I was nervous about how I would fit in. Mostly, I was nervous about how my game would translate at this level.

Walking in, I was happy to see two familiar faces from the open tryout speaking with the Director of Basketball Operations (DBO). A sense of relief came over me as I realized I would not be alone as the newly acquired walk-on. One of the guys I knew prior had also played high school ball in San Diego, and we had played together in an all-star game. He was a crafty undersized point guard, high basketball IQ, great shot. The other was a shooting guard from Los Angeles, a great mid-range shooter with excellent handles.

The first day involved filling out mandatory NCAA paperwork conducted by the head athletic trainer. We were told the paperwork would take a few days to clear. Until then, we were prohibited from taking part in practice, but the DBO emphasized we should sit together in the stands and watch its entirety to get a feel for what practice was actually like. More importantly, he wanted us to understand the team's dynamics before joining.

We took our seats way up in the shadows of our massive 12,000-seat arena; everything was pitch dark except for the vacant court, which shined under bright lights. Next to us were an assortment of journalists and a mix of visiting coaches from different parts of the state also there to observe. Two local news stations were courtside, setting up their cameras. I overheard a reporter saying the team was still watching film in the locker room. About 45 minutes later, some players began to trickle out of the locker room behind an assistant coach. As they began warming up and shooting around, the assistant coaches shook hands and chatted with nearby journalists and visiting coaches.

Coach Fisher came trotting out a few minutes after everyone else. It was wild how quickly the atmosphere in the arena changed. Small talk and friendly chatter among writers and managers stopped, and the on-court aura immediately changed to serious business and professionalism. It was just like in the movies when a CEO walks into the office and employees are suddenly extra attentive. It was interesting to see the similarities between the dynamics in high-level sports and boardroom meetings.

Before Coach could make it to the main circle on the court, he was intercepted by media and news reporters. After completing what seemed like a two-minute interview with multiple reporters, he strode to center court and blew his whistle. Everybody stopped shooting; not a ball hit the ground. Each player and assistant coach jogged toward the midcourt. Time for practice.

Players and staff huddled around Coach, who stood in the center of the logo, drawing the focus of everyone in the stadium. Silence overcame the entire arena, as if time had stopped. From my vantage, I could see Coach reading off a paper, but I was too far away to hear anything. I couldn't help but get goosebumps—this was all pretty big-time, and soon I would have the opportunity to be a part of it. Excited was an understatement.

When practice began, the players were split up on opposite sides of the court—big guys on one end, guards and wings on the other, each group managed by a designated coach. The high level attention to detail was impressive. Each section of practice had been critically developed to create the best flow possible. From a player standpoint, what stood out most was how the best players on the court operated with such detailed pace and consistent decision making. Every player on the court was extremely athletic, but what differentiated the best from average, was their ability to make accurate split-second decisions. They never seemed rushed, always played at their own speed, making the complexities of the game look simple, making everything look so easy. It was beautiful to watch.

The DBO came up and sat with us. He was a man of high character, an absolute gem of a human, but most importantly, he always treated everyone the same. That's a rare quality in athletics, and he won my utmost respect from the very start. He began telling us stories about each player—

who he was, where he was from, what he had accomplished. I knew the team had one returning walk-on in the program but didn't know who it was. The DBO pointed him out and told us to watch him closely as practice continued.

I observed his every move. In a couple days, I'd be in the same position. I wanted to be prepared when my time came. The weird thing was, practice was already halfway complete and the returning walk-on had yet to take part in a single drill. He had spent the entire time standing on the sideline. I wondered why… He hadn't even played in drills as elementary as layup lines. I was confused but didn't think too much of it. By the time the three-hour practice concluded, he had participated in only two drills: five minutes playing ball-screen defense and 10 minutes rebounding for the scholarship players. That was it. I thought, "Who knows? Maybe he's not feeling well. Maybe he's injured."

After a couple days of watching from the stands, I was officially cleared to practice. I was stoked. I could barely focus in class that morning and showed up at the arena an hour and a half early. My gear was waiting for me in my locker. I had my own jersey. It was surreal. I played it cool, though. Not wanting to make a big deal with my teammates around, I went into a bathroom stall to put on the jersey, then took a long pause to view myself in the mirror. I was officially a DI basketball player. It was an unbelievable feeling. I had checked the first box in a long list of personal goals. Excited? Nervous? Definitely. But I was also ready to practice and put in the work. I was prepared. I was confident.

I tied my shoes and hurried out to the court 45 minutes before practice would begin to do my normal shooting warm-up. When it was time, everything went through the exact same routine as before, except I was on the court. Coach blew his whistle; we all jogged to midcourt and huddled around him. He introduced us to the team and then gave a brilliant speech about the importance of mental toughness, extra effort, and doing what is best for the team: "The team, the team, the team."

My heart was pumping. I couldn't wait to get started. He ended his speech. Practice began. I'll never forget what happened next.

The first drill was the three-man-weave layup drill. The goal was to make 12 in a row. I went to the very back of the line and nervously awaited my turn even though it was a drill I'd been doing since I was eight years old. When I finally got to the front and it was my turn, out of nowhere an assistant coach yelled, "Hey! What is he doing in this drill? Get out! Scholarship players only!"

My heart stopped. I was confused, frazzled. I quickly apologized, stepped away, and stood on the sideline. What did I do wrong?

During a water break the DBO called me over with the other two walk-ons. "Just a reminder: Never be first in line for drills. Always try to ask a coach if they need any help; and if not, stand on the sideline until told otherwise."

I was so filled with adrenaline that I couldn't even

think. I just answered, "Yes, sir!"

Halfway through the same practice, not knowing any better, I naively hopped into a shooting drill. I had gotten kicked out of the first drill because it involved the entire team, but this drill was just for guards. I figured since it was a smaller group with fewer participants, this meant there was space for me to participate. Shooting was my best skill, so I knew I'd be able to perform at a high level. Halfway through running the drill perfectly, I was singled out again and kicked out by the coach in charge. I scurried over to the sideline, brushing it off with a false smile, but embarrassment coursed throughout my body.

The first practice lasted four hours. I had participated for 15 minutes—five minutes playing defense and 10 minutes of rebounding while others shot. The rest of the time I was on the sidelines watching scholarship players scrimmage. Day One: Four hours and I didn't shoot a single shot. Of course, I was disheartened. But it was only the first day. I was optimistic an opportunity would eventually present itself.

Still, after three weeks of four-hour practices in which I participated on average 10 minutes a day—not even getting close to breaking a sweat—I was feeling pretty low. Lower than I had ever felt before. Up to that point, basketball was something I had always felt confident about; it was something that united me with my teammates; it was my identity. I had never experienced anything like this. I didn't know how to handle these new emotions. All the energy, confidence, and prior excitement I'd had disappeared. I felt like I didn't belong.

Practice became less about basketball and more about fighting battles in my head over what drills I was allowed to participate in and what drills were solely for scholarship players. I'd be on the sideline replaying the scenes of humiliation in my mind. "Why is he in this drill?", "What are you doing?", "Someone, grab him!" I never wanted to experience any situations like that again. Sometimes, even if I did have an opportunity to compete in a drill, I'd subconsciously shy away from playing the game I loved. Not because I was incapable, but because the feeling of invisibility felt warmer than the cold humiliation.

After another month of this newfound reality, I realized there was definitely a lack of information about what being a collegiate walk-on actually entailed, nothing to help athletes navigate the newfound reality of living at the end of the bench. Instead of enjoying the game I had devoted my life to and the natural talents I had developed, I was on the sideline stuck in my head for four hours every day—my first cue on how fragile a young athlete's mental health can be. The sadness began to mask itself as overwhelming anxiety. It was as if I had never played basketball before, let alone been a successful high school player. In the back of my mind, I knew I couldn't be the only one struggling. But this was my new reality.

I knew complaining wouldn't change anything. I had to learn to adapt and make the most of any opportunity because, at the end of the day, being able to be at practice at all was just that: AN OPPORTUNITY.

"VALLEY OF TRANSITIONAL CRISIS"

Figure (1): Portrays the different phases of adapting to a new culture. Crisis is common in every transition. How does one integrate systems to be prepared for the upcoming emotional crisis that WILL occur?

*Source: (Cultural Adjustment | Berkeley International Office)

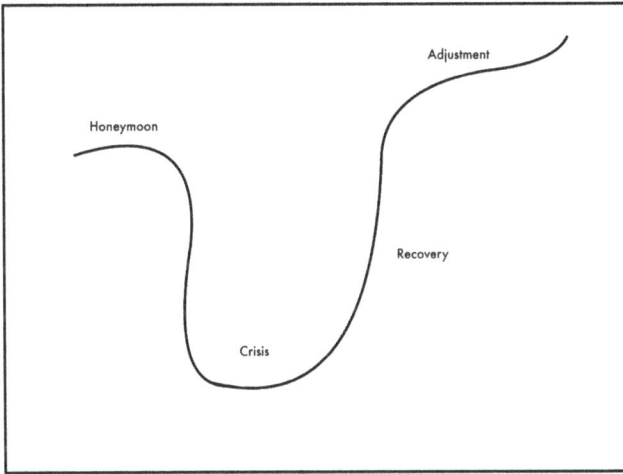

(KEY): Honeymoon: Making/Joining team.

Crisis: Transitioning from highly successful athlete to end of bench.

Recovery + Adjustment: Light,

The hardest part for me was being unable to travel to away games. Each time we'd finish practice before every road game, I'd see the suitcases packed and ready in my teammates' lockers while I'd be grabbing my stuff, wishing them good luck. Then, as they boarded the bus and headed off, I'd be heading in the opposite direction, back to my dorm room.

I started to think, "If I'm not traveling, am I even on the team?"

One of the main reasons I had initially decided to become a walk-on was my desire to become a part of something bigger than myself. A community. I knew the transition would take some getting used to, but the hardest adjustment was trying to feel connected with the team. In high school, when I had a major role, I never thought twice about *connection*. Our connection came from being on the floor and competing towards a common goal. Now I was sitting in the dark at the end of the bench, at the bottom of the depth chart.

I was in limbo. I'd feel like I belonged when we played home games, experiencing both the good and bad moments along with my teammates and staff. The connection was there. But as soon as the team left for an away game, it would all vanish, and I'd find myself back in the dark. Not traveling prevented me from experiencing those in-between moments that occur on the road, those indescribable instances that play such a profound role in developing a team's culture and forming bonds between players and staff. Each time the team would return from a road trip, practice felt like day one all over again. I was constantly struggling to re-establish myself into the culture.

> "Nothing sustains motivation better than belonging to the team, it transforms a personal quest into a shared one. Previously, you were on your own. When you join a team, your identity becomes linked to those around you. Growth and change is no longer an individual pursuit. The shared identity begins to reinforce your personal identity. Its friendship, team, and community that embed a new identity and help behaviors last over the long run."
> — James Clear, *Atomic Habits*
> (Clear, 2018)

I knew what I was missing, and I wanted to fix it.

My first year was an amazing year for the team. That season, led by Mountain West Conference (MWC) Player of the Year Xavier Thames, we had gotten as high as No. 5 in the nation, and finished the regular season at No. 10 in the AP Poll. We won the MWC regular-season title before losing in the conference tournament to New Mexico. We were still supposed to be weathering the departure of Kawhi Leonard. The season turned out to be a complete surprise to everyone.

I'd watched all our road games from my couch. I was grateful to be part of our team and to share in their success, but watching half of our games on TV really sucked. I thought things might be different once the NCAA

Tournament started. After all, the games were do or die, and the NCAA was funding everything. Surely, I thought, that meant the entire team would be traveling. Nope. When the team left, I was back at my dorm room.

We earned a No. 4 seed in the Tournament. The first two games were played in Dayton. We won an overtime thriller against New Mexico State in the Round of 64, then beat North Dakota State in the Round of 32 to reach the Sweet 16. The next matchup—against perennial powerhouse Arizona, which had defeated us in a tough game earlier in the season—would be played closer to home in Anaheim. Coincidentally, the biggest game of the year would also be the closest road game of the season, a short two-hour bus trip. My hopes rose again: Maybe I'd finally be invited to travel with the team.

Talk about HYPE. The media were calling it "the biggest game in the history of the program." Everybody was talking about this game. To be honest, I couldn't hardly wait either. I was praying day and night this would be my opportunity to travel.

When the team bus left for Anaheim, I wasn't on it. I tried not to show it, but I was devastated. Walking back to my dorm room, I couldn't help but question whether being a walk-on was worth it. Every time I got left behind, the community aspect I yearned for would seem less achievable.

Not traveling to this game was even more hurtful as a local, homegrown player. Every person I had grown up with was either going to Anaheim to watch the game in person or would be watching it on TV. This game hurt the most. The number of confused calls and texts I was receiving ("Are you there? Where are you, Niksha? I don't see you.") were taking their toll on me. My answer (excuse) to everybody was usually something like, "I'm just a freshman, and freshman walk-ons don't travel." It was a lie and a cop-out, but it was the only way I could disguise my insecurity over the situation.

I mean, was I even on this team? Sure, on paper I was, but was I really part of the team? I practiced every day, had my own jersey with my name on it, my own number. I suited up for home games, but inside I felt left out and overlooked.

Is this what it means to be a walk-on?

After waving goodbye to the team bus, I decided that I would go to my parents' house to hang out with my family for the night to take my mind off things.

My two best friends on the team were Angelo Chol and Parker U'u. After spending the night at my parents', they called me to work out with them on campus. Both were redshirt transfers, so they wouldn't travel with the team either (NCAA rules dictated that transfers had to sit out their entire first year at a new school). After our workout, we ate lunch together, and during our meal someone threw out the notion that we should just go to the game ourselves. Angelo, having just transferred from Arizona, got super excited about the idea. What began as a joke turned into the three of us contacting our DBO about coming to the game. He told us, if we manage to find a way there, he would get us in. I volunteered to drive us. Not only did I want to experience a Sweet 16 atmosphere, I wanted to prove to my friends, family, and skeptics I was actually on the team. I put $100 into the tank of my gas-guzzling truck, and we set off for the Honda Center in Anaheim.

We arrived about an hour before tipoff. There were already thousands of people outside of the arena. The energy was incredible—people of all sorts yelling, partying, and enjoying the thrill of cheering on their universities. March Madness!

From the moment we stepped out of the car, we stuck out like sore thumbs: three guys, 6'5", 6'7", 6'10", walking through the crowd, wearing team polos and dress pants. While waiting outside for our DBO, people were staring at us, pointing and whispering to their kids, "Look! Those guys are on the team." Finally, our DBO spotted us from afar, pointed us out to security, and we were let in through a VIP entrance. We were so excited to see our teammates and coaching staff... or so we thought.

Once inside, our DBO told us we were not allowed to be on the bench, but he had got us three tickets. We were a little shocked. After having driven over two hours on our own to support our squad, we definitely didn't think we'd be doing so from the bleachers. My two friends were upset, but they were both ineligible to play. I was on the roster, yet there I was in the stands watching my team play. That hurt.

It was a tightknit battle throughout, but in the end, Arizona was too much. Just like that, Season One was done. I was no longer a freshman. I could no longer use that as an excuse for not playing or not traveling with the team.

On the car ride home, while my friends were sleeping, a light switch flipped on in my head. I never wanted to have that feeling again of sitting in the stands and watching my team lose—all while losing a year of eligibility. I was going to give my all, day in and day out, to try to create positive changes. The experience of having to watch that game from the stands made me the person I am today. As disappointed, frustrated, and embarrassed as I was, not being able to suit up in Anaheim for the Sweet 16 was the best thing that ever happened to me.

I might not have realized it at the time, but that drive back from the Honda Center was the turning point in my career.

CHAPTER THREE

"Success comes from curiosity, concentration, perseverance, and self-criticism."
— Albert Einstein

Looking back, I believe it took me a full three years to learn how to grow and create opportunity for myself while at the bottom of the depth chart. Three years of at least five practices per week, at least four hours each day, maybe 15,000 hours of learning. The following rules are here to provide guidance to all aspiring walk-ons and underdogs currently attempting to break through the cage.

RULE NO. 1: EMBRACE INITIATIVE X INTELLECT.
In my opinion, college programs take walk-ons for two main reasons: (1) to have extra bodies for completing drills during practice like scout team, rebounding, defense, etc.; and (2) to bring up the team's cumulative GPA. So, hypothetically speaking, the first opportunity to differentiate yourself is to dominate in the classroom. Getting good grades from the start is the quickest way to gain respect from the coaches and immediately show your worth to the program.

Walk-ons, especially open-tryout walk-ons, must excel in

their studies. You're expected to have one of the highest (if not the top) GPAs on the team. This fact became more apparent to me after another walk-on who had made the team my first year got cut because he couldn't maintain his GPA. His on-court performance was solid, but when his grades fell, he was gone. I cannot emphasize this enough: The program already has enough players who can play basketball and struggle in the classroom. It doesn't need you for that.

From the moment classes begin, scholarship players are mandated to attend study groups, tutoring sessions, and organized check-ins. They get scheduled reminders from professionals working for the university. There's a system in place for their success. As a walk-on, you must take initiative to create this system for yourself.

I made it a priority to schedule meetings with the team academic advisor my first year. This led to a great relationship and a structured roadmap for academic success. She was an amazing person who helped me immensely. I would recommend doing the same: Academic advisors tend to be extremely nice, helpful people. More often than not, they would love to help you, but you have to prove to them that you care. This means taking ownership over your actions and SHOWING UP. Creating a system takes time, and it takes sacrifice. And brutal honest truth, as a walk-on you aren't "entitled" to anything within the program. You are not the priority, recognize this... The feeling of neglect can be channeled into a SUPERPOWER. Lean into it and use it as fuel. Your future self will thank you. It's up to you to decide what type of person you want to become. Nobody is going to choose for you. That's the beautiful aspect of being a walk-on, learning this uncomfortable truth positions you to THRIVE in the REAL WORLD.

RULE NO. 2: ATTITUDE: THE SKILL OF INVINCIBILITY
This rule might sound obvious, but positive attitude and body language is something every player can control. Like most things, it all comes down to ego management. It is a skill. If you can't put your ego aside to play the game you love, then all other rules are pointless.

In four years as a walk-on, some requests were near impossible to accept without negative emotions. Managing your ego is a constant battle. A prime example of *not* managing your ego is snapping at a teammate or coach and saying something you will certainly regret. We have all seen this happen. Don't let this be you.

Here's another example: During one practice, our scout team was told to run an opposing team's offensive scheme at "20-percent speed." Now, it was the day before our game, so there was no point in playing hard. However, while we were trying to run the play correctly at 20 percent, the scholarship players defended us at 100 percent. How do you think our execution turned out? Instead of assessing the real issue, the coaches immediately yelled at us for going too slowly.

We began to speed things up so we could actually execute

the play, and did so perfectly. The result? We got thrashed for playing too hard and running the offense too fast. How in the world is a basketball player supposed to know how to play at 20-percent speed? Some scholarship players on the sidelines were even laughing at us, but we were expected to stay quiet.

Situations like this occur daily, so be prepared for it. Staying quiet and keeping your cool is hard to do in the moment, but overall snapping back isn't worth it. Not talking back, not telling the coaches they're wrong is "the game inside of the game."

Don't get caught up in short-term right or wrong. Keep your focus on long-term growth. Living at the bottom of the depth chart will test you every day. Try your best to be aware of your emotions and keep them under control when you're on the court. Learning this tactic will lead to benefits far beyond sports.

That being said, I want to make it clear I am not saying you shouldn't stand up for yourself. Someone crossing the line and being disrespectful is far different than arguing over rights and wrongs in practice. Being friendly is important, but don't take disrespect from anyone. No matter how much power they have, stay true to your moral and ethical code and stand up for yourself if need be.

Every job has its own trials and tribulations. The subculture of collegiate athletics is no different. Some people will have "power trips" and knowingly or unknowingly make fun of you, put you down, or mistreat you. You have to know when to say enough is enough, and that's a very tricky threshold, whether you're on a basketball team or in an office setting. I bring this up only to keep you from being blindsided like I was.

Understanding how to control your own ego—and how to interact with others' egos—is a very important aspect to successfully operate within a larger collective.

RULE NO. 3: "STRATEGY OFTEN BEATS SWEAT."

Coaches bumped heads all the time over small details: how we walk-ons were playing, running a scout, or whether we should be participating in a drill. It was hard to tell why this happened. Was it because walk-ons had the smallest voices? To this day, I'm not sure, but it happened far too often.

Balancing out which coach to obey in practice was always something I struggled with, but I did learn this: Caught between two coaches, listen to whoever has more power. That means you have to carefully observe power dynamics and apply varying approaches. If one coach tells you to run a drill one way and then once the drill begins another coach tells you to run the drill a different way, listen to the more powerful coach. It might seem obvious. It's not. I can't stress how valuable your decision-making can be if you can stick to the food chain.

My first year, I didn't know any better. I listened to the opinions of every staff member on adjustments I should be making during practice. DO NOT DO THIS. You'll have a mess on your hands.

I'd start out by listening to whichever coach was running the drill. But then halfway through running the drill exactly as that coach wanted, another coach on the sideline would tell me I was doing it wrong and needed to do it his way. I'd make the adjustment, and then minutes later, the head coach might stop the entire drill, say I was doing everything completely wrong, and ask why I'd ever play like that. I'd find myself caught in the middle. Of course, the second coach, whose changes I'd implemented, would stay silent, and I'd be standing there alone, vulnerable.

After this happened numerous times, I got sick of it. By my fourth year as a walk-on, I had created a mental chart of the power differences between our five coaches. That allowed me to run drills "correctly" while saving myself from embarrassing moments and frequent headaches.

As a walk-on, you are tossed into a new team culture that has co-existed for years. It takes time to work your way into the fold.

* * *

Figure (2) ORGANIZATIONAL POWER CHART: Tailoring decision-making to vague power structures may allow you to maneuver confusion more clearly. Building momentum while at the bottom takes time. Focus on stacking small strategic breakthroughs.

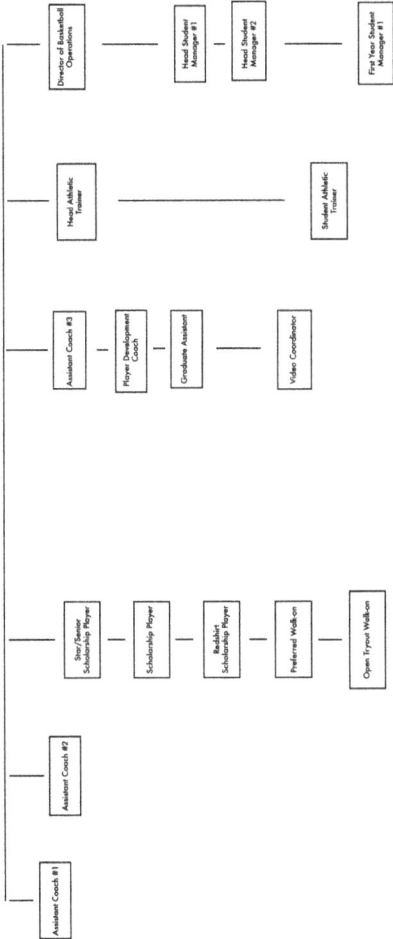

RULE NO. 4: "BECOME OBSESSED. BALANCE CAN COME LATER" - STEVE NASH

It didn't matter what the task was. If I was asked to rebound for another player, I would focus all my attention to dominate as the best rebounder on the court. If I was told to portray an opposing player on scout team, I was going to be that *exact* player. If I was told to grab waters and bring them to the bench, I grabbed the waters as quickly as possible and brought them with a smile on my face. Once my perspective changed, my mindset followed. I became more determined every day I stepped foot on the court. I stared reality in the face. I decided what type of person I wanted to be. I stayed engaged, rather than disconnected. I came to terms with my situation and started chipping away to make the most of it. I convinced myself that, even if all the extra effort failed to amount to more playing time, at least I would know I had given it my all. And you know what? Parts of practice I used to dread, started to become fun.

As a walk-on in any arena of life, if you can apply this perspective from the beginning, you might be surprised just how quickly you see results.

CHAPTER FOUR

"Make sure your worst enemy doesn't live between your own two ears."
— Laird Hamilton

Building awareness of my mental health and performance anxiety was the most important adjustment I made to emerge out of the intense dark cage of weak identity I had associated myself with.

Anxiety, in general, is a consistent theme throughout this book—that's because an extremely difficult aspect of being at the end of the bench is dealing with newfound anxiety.

As years of being treated like a second-class player on the team stacked up, so did my anxiety. It was paralyzing. Over my first two years, rather than acknowledge my anxiety, I'd fight it, and that only made it worse. I didn't know who to talk to—I mean, who would be able to relate? I had played basketball my entire life without experiencing any of these new emotions. I had gone from arguably one of the best in San Diego to not being allowed into elementary drills. That was a hard transition; it took a mental toll on me.

Mostly, my anxiety confused me. It seemed ridiculous. How could playing the sport that I loved lead to performance anxiety? It made no sense to me.

As a walk-on, everything got more complicated, and my perspective on the game changed. With each passing practice and game, I was becoming more self-critical. Instead of playing the game naturally, like I had always done, I began to play with a sense of self-doubt and rigidness. My private inner voice became louder and more negative than ever.

There's a stigma surrounding the topic that I want to shatter.

Where did this negative voice suddenly come from?

I was putting immense hours into my game behind the scenes, improving my weaknesses—all for one chaotic minute to play perfect, to change everyone's perception. To change my perception. If I was lucky, I might get one shot. If I missed, it was as if all the hours of practice and any improvement I'd seen weren't real. And if I made that shot, it meant nothing—the game was over, and there was zero chance of showcasing further.

> *"The power broker in your life is the voice that no one hears. How well you revisit the tone and content of your private voice is what determines the quality of your life. It is the master storyteller, and the stories we tell ourselves are our reality."*
> — Dr. Jim Loehr

Performance anxiety is unhealthy and unhelpful, but not uncommon—it's a phenomenon that every athlete experiences to some degree. However, athletes have a really hard time discussing performance anxiety or depression because it forces them to reveal their vulnerabilities. It forces them to prioritize seeking help, rather than "pushing through", an uncomfortable and unfamiliar territory for a high-level athlete.

Growing up athletes have always had coaches tell them to "push through" a situation and their great ability to do so, has led to positive outcomes, praise, or wins.

"Pushing through" = Positive Association = Win, Strong "Asking for help" = Negative Association = Giving up, Weak

But with mental fitness and well-being this "push through" phenomenon comes with limitations. At times, it might serve us better to substitute "pushing through" for "seeking help". Implementing a more balanced approach to your complex situation could help ease some of the mental tension. It is no easy task to evaluate this alone, so seeking help may be the unpopular solution.

"Don't be ashamed to need help. Like a soldier storming a wall, you have a mission to accomplish. And if you've been wounded and you need a comrade to pull you up? So what?"
— Marcus Aurelius, Meditations (1)

Diving deeper into this topic, is Dr. Oliver Eslinger, a top researcher at the forefront of sport and performance psychology, neuroscience, and mental conditioning. *Dr. Eslinger* is the current Head Men's Basketball Coach at Caltech (14 years), worked at MIT (6 years) and received his doctorate in counseling psychology with a specialization in sport psychology from Boston University. Doc's vision is clear: with an extreme focus on mental performance, he wants to create a championship program with the world's most brilliant student-athletes. Dr. Eslinger's interests include cognitive behavioral mechanisms of training and performance, mental imagery ability, and processes involved in decision making.

Dr. Eslinger:
"I imagine being a walk-on embodies walking a metaphorical and paradoxical fine line of having to be tight and loose at the same time, all the time. Sitting there, watching, wondering, lost in thought, knowing almost for certain you won't hear your name called to check into the game. Yet you can't be so loose you become a distraction to the team. One's mindset has to be focused and ready to provide help and energy however

see fit — otherwise what's the point of you being there? Your concentration is tight — it's on the team and the game. Heck, you might even have to fetch a towel or water for a teammate. Or hold a clipboard for a coach. To be seen as an asset, it's a "by any means necessary" profile. All the while, in your soul, you know you do want to play. To prove you belong, that you can play, that you have the skills to make an impact on the court. And maybe one day even earn a scholarship."

The racing thoughts, the dreaming, imagining, toying with scenarios — the strings and snowballing of notions can hit on the spectrum of cognitive anxiety. The main question to ask is: What are you telling yourself? Because the thoughts lead to stories. And the more stories conjured from your thoughts, which can come in the form of words or phrases or images, add up to a book of cognitions. One word, phrase, image leads into the next and can trigger a sequence of doubt, discomfort, and fear, setting the stage for a consistent state of anxiety where it almost feels like it's you. And then not having the coping skills to deal with these negative thoughts can lead into other issues like depression, distress, and disillusioned thinking.

But that's not all — jumping from anxious thought to anxious thought can also make one feel lousy. The physiological mechanisms involved in anxiety can be interpreted as negative as well, especially when one feels off. Butterflies or an upset stomach. Sweaty and overheated. The somatic impact revolves from feelings back to thoughts and in combination can create alternative actions where one really feel like he is spiraling out of control. The anxious thoughts and feelings begin to impact one's next thoughts and feelings and without proper mental solutions one can work himself into a frenzy. How can I do this? What will they think of me? I feel like I've lost everything! Well, I'm not good enough anyway and I feel like a nervous wreck. I'm just a walk-on.

And there lies the problem with the label. The limiting label of being named something by others so that others can continue to look at you and interpret you as something else, one who doesn't fit the rest. You have a title and it doesn't go along with what the rest of the team looks and feels like which can only add to how you're processing the entire situation. Always trying to be better, to prove, to demonstrate your work ethic and commitment to the team is much more than anyone knows. Even when you're not allowed to practice. Or attend a team event. Or sit with the team at the game! The challenge lies in front of you. Your identity is what you make of it, not what others say you are. But how to muster the strength to mute the noise in and around you? That's where the mental skills, the proper coping mechanisms come into play.

The ability to self-regulate to stay in the moment and enjoy the entire experience is the key. Learning how to breathe, to relax, to imagine proper actions and responses, to process thoughts, feelings, and behaviors in positive ways with positive outcomes. Interpreting all as a challenge and understanding the stress response is inherent in humans — it's our nature to want more and when we want more we care more. If we didn't care about the goal, we wouldn't think about it so much. We wouldn't feel it so much. We wouldn't behave as if we wanted it. I've often said the phrase: Fear is like fire. IF you control it, it'll cook for you. If you don't harness it, it will burn you. It's not about getting rid of the fear or exterminating the feelings and thoughts accompanying it — it's about working with it. Our brains are wild things — taking in so much all the time, some conscious, much of it filtering through the subconscious. Ultimately, our inner workings are about survival — what do I need right now to keep on keeping on? Fear can focus you. The anxious thoughts and feelings are a signal alerting us to what we have to focus on and what we do indeed care about. Efficiency self-awareness skills come into play as we integrate mental techniques from our resilience toolbox. Noticing our emotions. Our cognitions. Our actions. And then breathing to a point where we are at a workable performance zone ready to take on whatever comes our way. A walk-on grapples with the unknown. You have to become comfortable being uncomfortable. Each player is a vehicle. And some are going to be seen as sports cars and others are going to be seen as four wheels and a body taking up space.

Where others may label you as an outsider, you can use that as motivation. Rev yourself up like the most efficient and well-built car engine, and become the Ferrari."

"MENTAL FITNESS REBOOT"

NF: What are some proactive steps a person can take to allow their anxiety to work for them?

Dr. Eslinger: Awareness is the top priority. But only through mental practice can one become accustomed to how he or she feels in a good state, or a high-powered controllable form, ready to respond and perform. It takes a lot of practice and reflection but by incorporating mindfulness, or other forms of thought and feeling training, a person can reach a new level of understanding. Both internally and externally, one can learn to identify their moods, needs, and triggers. With various breathing and imagery routines, self-talk, journaling, and re-framing strategies, a person can translate their cognitions and emotions into a systematic form of art. In fact, as we know from science and how humans have evolved, anxiety is a good thing -- it can help us focus, motivate, and allow us to perform in ways that may have otherwise been dormant. It's almost like having a superpower if we access and assess in developmental ways.

NF: When transitioning from a large role, to spending vast amount of time at the "end of the bench", what are the different types of anxieties of which to be aware of?

Dr. Eslinger: Transitions of any kind can be stressful. It's the unfamiliarity with new scenarios and overall uncertainty that can cause various anxieties. In effect, we are talking about change and how to manage the emotions associated with novel and stressful situations. Cognitive anxiety, which entails thoughts and images we experience, is powerful. Our cognitions tell us a story and if the story is full of anxious notions that lead to emotions like doubt and fear, performance can be hindered. Somatic anxiety is experienced physiologically, as in the feelings athletes have in their bodies. Muscle tightness, dry mouth, sweating profusely, inability to sit still -- all sorts of nervousness that can lead to severe discomfort. Even more, athletes can behave in ways not normal for their character -- like having more of a short fuse, or not listening appropriately, and experiencing a variety of distracting ideas.

NF: How can a person improve their inner voice and response systems to anxieties or mistakes?

Dr. Eslinger: Start with watching or imagining performance. Good and bad. Positive and negative. When it went your way and when it didn't. Write descriptions of what is going on, the thoughts and the feelings. Get it down on paper and out of your head. Compare the examples. Too often we exaggerate or catastrophize without getting the entire chapter down -- all the details. How it actually went. With debriefing and analyzing the entire performance we get a more realistic picture of reality. Now -- with the good stuff, tap more into it. How to maximize the great thoughts and feelings -- those that lead to recurring positive self-talk and inspirational imagery. And with the bad -- change one word or sentence and restructure the negative into a flexible and meaningful sentence, as if taking the next turn, the next step. It's not a loss, it's a lesson. We can choose how we respond. And the more control we have over decision techniques, because of our alertness and coping skills, we can learn to manage and respond in really powerful ways.

NF: When entering a new environment, how can people improve on their inner voice while clearly at the bottom of the food chain?

Dr. Eslinger: Take it step by step. Lesson to lesson. Day to day. Write out a plan. Imagine it. Act as if. The mind doesn't know what's real or not -- we make it that way. Dreams sometimes feel very real, right? We daydream, too, and can get lost in those emotions. We can make the environment what we want with our thought patterns and how we interpret feelings. You can't go from a 1 to a 10. But you can go from 1 to 2. Then a 2 to a 3, and so on. Keep the long-term vision in mind and on paper. But focus on the little things that will become the big things. Ask questions. Engage in the process. Build sweat equity. Be ready for your chance.

NF: While at the "end of the bench", how does one re-frame his or her identity to lead towards better performance?

Dr. Eslinger: Again, it's the power of story and the words and images we create and perceive. It's easy to get lost in a monotonous pattern of saying things and doing things that only add to a struggle -- but what if you are able to change it all, manipulate it in a way where you get one percent better each day? Say it, do it, review it, and do it all again. Athletes have to imagine all types of scenarios. When action is going well and how to maintain it, or even elevate it. And when things aren't going well -- understand how to respond, how to eliminate or decrease errors, get back into a good rhythm or thought and feeling. Behave how you want to behave -- as in, if you were going to tell your story in 10 years, how does it look and what are the trends?

NF: What specific proactive steps can be incorporated into an athlete's game-day routine to help conquer newly found performance anxiety struggles?

Dr. Eslinger: First, recognize how and when you feel at your best. Sleep, nutrition, and human interactions all matter and influence performance. The ability to organize your life is crucial -- it prevents and deletes clutter. Second, behave in a way that puts you in a positive pattern intentionally and consistently. By practicing perfectly you become alert to any changes in thoughts and feelings – those changes become more noticeable. Music is a terrific and accessible trigger. Video and images provide sensations and memories through our eyes -- by paying attention to what we see we can adapt and activate very quickly. Forms of mindfulness can be integrated into daily routines, pre-games, and halftimes. And certainly reflection is a cool down piece often disregarded -- spend time on what went well and what was learned.

CHAPTER FIVE

"Making the best of what we do have, instead of begrudging what
we don't, has a way of creating all that we'll ever need."
— Charles F. Glassman

Instead of trying to revolutionize everything in my life, I decided I was going to make tiny tweaks in various areas with the hopes that they would translate to something different on the basketball court. Two years later, as I scribble all this down on a professional basketball contract, I can humbly say: These tiny tweaks did change my life.

Tiny Tweaks ➔ Big Changes
- Amy Cuddy

TINY TWEAK NO. 1: NO, AS A STRATEGIC YES.
Everything begins with mindset. I decided that, when I was on the court, there was no holding back. Sure, my teammates were some of my best friends, but everything inside the lines was a battle. All I saw was the game.

For my first two years as a walk-on, I was too preoccupied about fitting in and being friends with the guys on the team. Many times, I would take plays off because my teammates asked me to. I wanted to be a good teammate and even a better friend, so I would comply. As a walk-on—and this applies to anyone lower on the ladder—knowing when to defer to your coaches and teammates and when to do what is best for yourself becomes one of the hardest lines to draw.

My first experience with this delicate boundary came during the third practice of my first year. My assignment was to defend the post against one of our star players. It was just a drill, but many of our coaches were watching. No one expected me to be able to guard him. He was an upperclassman, stronger, easily one of the best players on the team.

When he caught the ball on the right block and began to post me up, I bumped him once, knowing in my head he would try to go middle. He took the bait, attacked the middle with his right hand. As he rose for the layup, I timed it perfectly and volleyball-spiked the ball out of bounds. A shocked "Ooh!" arose from everyone watching. I heard an assistant coach saying, "Damn, Niksha, didn't think you had that in you."

I'd surprised myself, too. It felt good!

The very next play, my teammate posted me up again, same spot—except this time, before he got the ball, he said, "Bro, relax…it's just a drill. Don't go so hard." Having a senior player tell me this put me in an uncomfortable position. I knew I should ignore him, but also as a new kid on the team I didn't want to cause any problems. So, that next play, I eased up and let him score.

Had I known then what I would realize later, I should have ignored him. Holding back kept me from demonstrating my value and climbing the ladder. While it's important to assimilate into the culture, you HAVE to be aware of when to draw that line for yourself. When to say NO, is just as important as YES.

TINY TWEAK NO. 2: "USE THE BAD TO FUEL THE GOOD." — STEVEN KOTLER

While residing at the bottom of the D1 athlete food chain, applying this tweak helped me climb higher. Instead of giving up or feeling bad for myself, I used all those negative emotions to my advantage. I held this idea close to my heart, pinned it to my shoulder, and used it to attack every day that would follow. That fuel propelled me to take authority over the decisions I had made and would make.

I considered myself one of the best shooters on the team, but I was not allowed to shoot during shooting drills in practice. Probably one of the most frustrating aspects of being a walk-on was rebounding for scholarship players for four entire years.

The drill was straightforward. A player shoots 3-pointers for one minute. If he makes at least five in a row, he yells out his name, and Coach would then yell out that player's name and the number of consecutive shots he'd made. This would go on for 10 minutes.

I am proud of my shooting ability, so I was confident

this was a drill where I could really show what I could do. I could make five or more 3-pointers with ease. So, rebounding for 10 minutes straight without being able to get one shot up was hard on my soul.

After two-and-a-half years of minimal-effort re-bounding, I finally made a tiny tweak that would help me make the most of my situation. Instead of just going through the motions during those 10 minutes, I expanded my frequency and channeled it towards personal improvement.

Each basket had three people shooting simultaneously, which meant at least four balls were in the air at once. I began to play my own game, challenging myself to time each rebound perfectly by predicting the angle a miss would take coming off the rim. I would lock in on one specific player's shot, and my goal was to make sure—amid the chaos of all the other shots—that I prevented this one ball from touching the floor. I figured if I did this every day, I'd improve at the art of rebounding.

My tiny tweaks had turned something I disliked into a path to exponential growth. I became a far better rebounder by doing this.

TINY TWEAK NO. 3: SEEK A NEW PERSPECTIVE.
Walk-ons often spend a big part of practice standing on the sidelines, waiting to be told to rebound or play defense. It's easy to get lost staring into space when you're hardly ever involved. Instead of getting upset over this reality, I decided

I would focus all my energy on what the coaches were telling the starters and other players who got heavy minutes. After a while, this enhanced focus turned into expanded awareness of coach's trends and preferences.

The most important thing I noticed? If a coach stops practice to correct one of your teammates on something they have done wrong in a drill, you better make sure you don't make that same mistake when it's your turn! That is every coach's pet peeve.

Observing most practices from the sidelines provided me with more of a coach's perspective. Everything started to make more sense. Analyzing drills helped me become more detail-oriented and realize the importance of running drills exactly as coaches wanted. I could see how crucial mistakes in practice affected the coaching staff's overall trust in a player, and how that correlated to the playing time a player received in game situations. I was receiving higher education. Employing a coach's perspective while on the court can pave the way for increased opportunities.

TINY TWEAK NO. 4: SCOUT TEAM: THE ART OF BEING POSITIONLESS

For those who might not know, scout team is when a group of players, normally walk-ons and players on the bench, imitate future opponents' tendencies during practice to prepare the starters for games. Scout team is and will always be the most important job as a walk-on.

Looking back, I believe scout team played the biggest role in my growth as a basketball player. When I got to SDSU, I had a one-dimensional IQ. I had always seen the game through the eyes of a long-range shooter. That's who I am, who I've always been, and who I will always be. Scout team forced me to reset my programming. Were there hiccups in the beginning? Absolutely. As a freshman, scout team was frustrating because I felt like my biggest strength was always being neutralized. I'd often get assigned roles that highlighted my weaknesses instead of my strengths. Rather than having an attitude about it, I embraced it.

A huge wake-up call.

Being a member of the scout team was giving me thousands of hours of data to learn new sets, new players, new ways to play basketball. It was teaching me how to have the awareness to dissect and efficiently adapt my game. It was teaching me how to be positionless.

Taking on the role of a different player each week obligated me to step out of my comfort zone and play through my weaknesses. Frequently, I'd be roleplaying an opposing team's slasher, forcing me to scrimmage through a new lens. Suddenly, I was attacking the rim like a completely different player, shooting floaters in the paint. I was attempting moves I never would have dared had I already established a role as "Niksha Federico, 3-point specialist." If I started playing my game—hovering outside and dropping 3s—coaches would yell at me. So long as I played my part, there were no repercussions.

More importantly, though, in the long run competing as a different player helped me reach a higher ceiling than I had ever thought possible. I had been handed a critical opportunity to get real-life data on how to improve weaknesses in my game without any consequences of failing. I got better at driving, seeing angles, and using different dribble moves to get to the rim. The player known as "Niksha Federico" was developing a new skillset. He was learning the ability to see beyond predefined positions and embrace complexity. He was re-learning how to learn. Seeing the improvements manifest increased my buy-in and raised my level of enjoyment. I got excited wondering what I'd be adding to my game that next week.

Scholarship players often work on their weaknesses after practice, through one-on-one coaching instruction. That's great but having the opportunity to focus on your weaknesses in live competition is invaluable. That's what the scout team provides—you are *forced* to hone in on your weaker skills but without the added pressure of failing.

Think outside the box and try to be the best scout team player in the nation.

HOW CAN YOU CREATE YOUR OWN TINY TWEAKS TO MAKE AN UNDESIRABLE SITUATION MORE DESIRABLE?

"SPEAKING TO THE PAST, TO HELP FULFILL THE FUTURE."

1. HAVE A LONG-TERM VISION. REDSHIRT DURING FRESHMAN YEAR.

Had I known that I could have redshirted going into my first year as a walk-on, my collegiate career would have been very different. Redshirting during your freshman year might be one of the best long-term decisions you'll have the opportunity to make for yourself. Saving a season of eligibility while still being able to graduate in four years are clear benefits. Yet, more importantly, redshirting during your first year will provide you an opportunity to strengthen your game and body during a crucial period of transition in your playing career.

Of course, my story was a bit different because I didn't truly understand the power and freedom that redshirting during my first year could have afforded me. No one thought to tell me that walk-ons even had the option (or were even allowed) to redshirt when I made the team my freshman year. I figured only scholarship players could make that decision. Lost in the incredible feeling of getting my own jersey, I would soon learn that I wouldn't be traveling with the team and played a total of 10 minutes that entire season. Just like that, my first year of eligibility was over and gone.

In the four years as a student athlete, you have control over very few circumstances. Redshirting is one of them. In almost every other instance, the coaches have complete control, and you better listen! But the ability to redshirt is your decision alone, so don't let anyone take it away from you.

Think long and hard and really consider your decision… Suiting up as a freshman walk-on is exciting short-term, but that chance will still be there the following year. I hate to be the bearer of bad news, but unless a few scholarship guys in your position get injured, chances are you will not be playing significant minutes as an unrecruited freshman walk-on.

So, redshirt. Save your eligibility. Get stronger in the weight room. Adapt your game to the speed and pace of college basketball. You might be extremely surprised to find out how much more comfortable you'll feel going into your second year.

Even though I didn't redshirt until my senior year, had I not redshirted, I never would have had the chance to go pro.

2. FIND YOUR *WHY*.

If you're in it solely for the gear, you won't last. You've got to love the game. Sorry if that's a rude awakening, aspiring walk-ons.

Before tryouts, students see athletes strutting around

campus in exclusive university athletic gear—cool sweatshirts, slick shorts, fancy backpacks, etc. Students covet that stuff. I've been there myself. I have felt the benefits, too. You feel like all eyes are on you as you walk around campus. It's especially nice for non-starters and walk-ons because students see you as part of something bigger. No one knows if you got reamed out in practice that morning, if you missed every shot that afternoon, if you never even participated in a single drill. All they see is the gear and the ambiance that comes with it. And that feels good.

During my freshman year, before I made the team, I really wanted an official team backpack. In my eyes, I felt the backpack would fill me with that sense of *belonging* again that had disappeared after graduating from high school. I also thought that the gear represented a sense of athletic accomplishment and prestige.

A regular student might see the fancy "free" athletic gear and say things like, "I'm so jealous," or, "That's so cool—must be nice." In reality, students don't see what happens behind the scenes. That gear means a lot less after a couple months of grinding five-hour practices—especially as a walk-on, when most of your time has been spent as a defender or rebounding for scholarship players or just standing on the sideline.

You have to find your why. What makes the most sense for you? What does the gear represent for you? Respect? Prestige? Athletic accomplishment? Belonging? Identity?

Material? Gear can be one reason you want to be a walk-on, but it cannot be your only reason. You still need the drive to play. You need to love the game. I'm telling you now: If you're in it for the gear, you will not last.

3. BE SPECIFIC ABOUT WHAT YOU BRING TO THE TABLE. BE AN ASSET ON THE COURT.

It has taken me six years of playing high-level basketball to fully understand the importance of being specific about the role you fill with your game. Growing up, we are taught to have "all-around games." You might hear things like:

"You're a great shooter, but you need to work on your dribbling."

Or...

"You're a great defender, but you need to work on your shooting."

What this can create, though, is a young, anxious basketball player who worries they will lose time on the court if they cannot improve these "weaknesses" in their game.

I believe that this concept loses its purpose once you get past the high-school level. For a walk-on, working to develop into an all-around player could delay opportunity. Instead, the focus should be to assess what is missing on the team and specialize in it. A true asset to the team.

Updated Definition:
Walk-on: Might not be athletic enough, but never outsmarted.
"Appreciate your position but plan your promotion."

Let's take a pause and be real here. Those already on scholarship have a head start on becoming better all-around players. Most likely, they have already grown into their bodies and have higher athleticism, talent, and skill across their entire game. I'm not saying this is always the case—there are exceptions.

Coaches tend to have a general four-year vision for each player they have recruited hoping that, with the right guidance and instruction, a recruit will become a star player. The reality is, maybe one of four incoming freshmen is likely to become a "star" and/or team leader by their senior year—that player who encompasses everything the coach envisioned when they recruited them back in high school. What happens to the other three players? Well, they received the same instruction, same guidance, but maybe they didn't develop completely or weren't as lucky. Maybe they got surpassed at their position by a younger recruit, leading to less playing time year by year. Since those players have been told to focus their energy on improving all aspects of their game, they become jacks of all trades instead of masters of one.

As a walk-on, it might make little sense to compete in a race when you have a weight tied to one foot. That doesn't mean winning is impossible. Many walk-ons have won, and many walk-ons will continue to do so. But please hear me out: What if the narrative was changed a bit? Instead of being one of the rare players who develop an all-around game after four years, what if you could become the *best* player at one specific skill and fill that niche for your team? Suddenly, a walk-on would no longer be competing against a dozen scholarship players but against maybe only one or two players who are supposed to fill that role as well.

If those players are also on scholarship, the coaches may be trying to make them complete packages in the hopes they can mold at least one of them into a "star."

Another thing to consider is that recruited players are promised different circumstances. Many were sold "dreams" to get them to commit to a program. You have made the team yourself— use that to your advantage. No one told you how you must play and there is no pressure of becoming a great player. So, it is easier for you to observe the team's dynamics, identify what is missing, and work on filling that role. With this mindset, by junior or senior year, I am almost certain you will have a higher chance to be better at that given role than any underclassmen would be, regardless of their scholarship status.

For example, I am a natural shooter and scorer, tall for my position, and have the ability to make tough shots. This was my game and how I played coming out of high school. However, after finishing my rookie year as a professional, I have come to the realization that being an efficient and successful scorer is a very hard task. The higher the level, the lower the odds of being able to be one of the best general scorers.

What if I hadn't tried to become a great scorer and all-around player like everybody else? What if I asked myself, "What can I be *best* at?"

If I could be a freshman walk-on again, I would have focused all my energy to be the best at corner 3-pointers, the best at offensive rebounding, and the best at not turning the ball over—that would have turned me into an immediate asset for any winning team. Notice the difference?

Back then, as a young walk-on, I didn't know any better. Nobody was in my corner giving me advice on how to train or how I should play, so I just mimicked what the coaches would tell the scholarship players and tried to do exactly that to the best of my ability. This approach limited my potential. Instead of getting an opportunity to play my second or third year as a walk-on, it took me four years to even get noticed.

So, change your perspective. Update the programming in your mind. The majority will be heading right while you will be going left. You may really be competing against only a few players, if that. Think long-term goals over short-term gratification.

"Don't over-improve your weaknesses. If you're not good at something, work on it until it no longer prevents your progress, but the bulk of your time is better spent maximizing your strengths."
— James Clear, *Atomic Habits*

Be aware of what skills you already have and where you're naturally better than other players. Then focus all your energy and attention on fine-tuning and sharpening these skills. If you can do that, there may be no stopping you.

4. PROUDLY BE YOURSELF. BE 1/1. LIVE YOUR STORY.

Be you, and be proud to be you.

As a first-year walk-on, everything is brand new. You are away from home for the first time. You have a new coaching staff and new teammates. You are constantly having to adapt to new environments. It can be easy to get caught up in trying to do and act like others.

I would tell my 18-year-old self to focus less energy on trying to be like the others and more on trying to become aware of his own habits. I would tell him, "Even though your sport may seem like the most important duty in your life—and it's how you identify yourself in this moment—try not to sweat it too much." I would remind him that life is bigger than basketball, and at the end of the day, it is just a game. The main goal is to be generally happy. No one needs to understand you, but you.

Embrace yourself. Be confident in who you are, and do you!

5. "LONELINESS IS A KIND OF TAX YOU HAVE TO PAY TO ATONE FOR A CERTAIN COMPLEXITY OF MIND." - ALAIN DE BOTTON

If you are reading this exact sentence, it is an incredible sign. It means somewhere deep down inside there is a want, a need, to make a change and grow out of the internal or external cage your inner voice has built. Eliminate all external distractions, and design time to think. Nothing can affect your confidence when you know who you are. Lean into this feeling, and channel the energy to continue the pursuit of molding into the best version of yourself.

CHAPTER SIX

"A dream written down with a date becomes a GOAL. A goal broken down into steps becomes a PLAN. A plan backed by ACTION makes your dreams come true."
— Greg Reid

Today, everything is digital. Few people tend to write with actual pens in actual notebooks. The more books I read about successful individuals, though, the more I noticed how many suggested the importance of physically journaling and writing down affirmations. It seemed like every book swore by it.

After class one day, I thought maybe I should try out this affirmation thing. What did I have to lose? At the time, I was heading into my third year on the team, and very little had changed. I still hadn't traveled to one away game, and I'd only seen the court for the last two minutes when the team was up by 20. Deep down I knew I was making big strides in my game, but in the public eye I still had nothing to show for it.

So, one day I walked into the local market and picked out a notebook and a pen to use solely for writing down affirmations. I remember being embarrassed as I paid the cashier.

Right before bed that night, I grabbed the notebook and pen from the plastic bag and wrote:

I, Niksha Federico, will...

The instructions I was following said to write down your name and then exactly what you envision for yourself. You were then supposed to write the same sentence a total of 15 times. In that moment, I desperately wanted to travel with the team—nothing more, nothing less. I just wanted to travel. So, I wrote:

I, Niksha Federico, will travel to away games.

Writing this became a habit. Every night before bed, I would secretly pull out the notebook so my roommate wouldn't see, and I would write the same sentence down 15 more times. Then I'd hide the notebook and go to sleep.

Once conference season had started and the first away-game travel list came, I wasn't on it. I was bummed, but I kept writing. Five months passed. Then my affirmation came to life.

My junior year, the team had a strong overall record and solid NCAA Tournament résumé. All was left was to play the Mountain West Conference tourney in Las Vegas—something I had always wanted to play in but had yet to have that chance.

One of my best friends at school would travel to the conference tournament every year with his family, which was all pretty ironic considering he was a non-athlete and I had never once attended. When the time came, he was reporting from there as I cheered on my team from home, watching on TV.

We won the first two games, but ended up losing in

the finals to a Fresno State team that was much better than it had performed during the season. The win earned them an automatic bid to the NCAA Tournament while officially putting us on the bubble.

Many people wonder what it's like for bubble teams on Selection Sunday. After experiencing it firsthand, I can say it's an energy unlike anything I had ever felt before. Nothing but nerves and anxiety. The previous two years, our team was in the Top 25, guaranteeing us a spot. During those years on Selection Sunday, our arena would be filled with fans excited to find out how we'd be seeded, where we'd end up playing, and who we'd draw as an opponent. It was a *huge* party. This year was different. No party. No fan-filled arena. No media. Just our team together in the locker room, nervous and unsure what the future held. Everything was up in the air.

Some TV analysts had us as the last team in; others had Syracuse. It was a coin toss. Forty-five minutes later… BOOM! Syracuse. We sat there and watched the entire bracket unfold with our team's name nowhere on it. The thrill of March Madness vanished. Straight crickets. Nobody said a word or moved a muscle. Maybe five minutes went by that felt like a century until SMACK! A senior with his head down slammed his hand into his locker bench and said, "Man, this is some BULL!" and stormed out of the locker room.

But when one door closes, another opens. Immediately after Selection Sunday, the National Invitation Tournament

(NIT) selection special follows. Our name popped up as a 2-seed.

Many players call the NIT the "Not-In-The-Tournament" tournament. Don't get me wrong—the NIT is a prestigious event and being selected is definitely something to be proud of. However, for a team who a week earlier had high hopes of a NCAA Tournament Cinderella run, it was a disappointment. In fact, many of my teammates were so disappointed they said they were done and would not play in the NIT.

It took a couple days of convincing to get the team motivated to play. Coach Fisher being the legend he is, though, knew exactly how to get his players' attention: New York. At the time, the "Final Four" of the NIT was being played in Madison Square Garden—one of the most legendary basketball venues in the world.

Growing up on the West Coast, playing at MSG seemed far-fetched unless you made it to the NBA. Coach used this to rally the spirits of the entire squad. "Three wins," he told us. "All we have to do is win three games, and we'll be playing at Madison Square Garden." Opportunity of a lifetime.

Long story short, we ended up pulling out those three games against three very solid teams—IPFW, Georgia Tech, and Washington—and there we were. Ticket punched. I was happy, but also a bit jealous. I still hadn't traveled to a single away game. Now at the end of my third year in the program, I knew better than to get my hopes up.

A couple days before the team was scheduled to depart, I received a text out of the blue from our DBO: "Any interest in traveling to NY? Coach said you're in."

Exactly five months after I began writing affirmations every night, my goal had finally become a reality. The years of hard work, dedication, perseverance, and positivity had paid off. Saying I was excited is an understatement!

Traveling with the team to New York was an unforgettable experience. Madison Square Garden was incredible! Though we would lose that next game to an extremely disciplined George Washington University team, the exposure was something I'll never forget. The entire trip had fanned the spark of belief in a kid who needed every ounce of confidence boost he could get. It was the first small win I had obtained in three years. I was ecstatic. Being able to see positive results finally come out of years of hard work jumpstarted a state of momentum that still carries me to this day.

CHAPTER SEVEN

"The secret to success was being ready for your opportunity when it presents itself...until then pay your dues."
— Benjamin Disraeli

This quote sums up what it means to be a walk-on. Many dues must be paid—and I'm not talking just tuition. Time. Sacrifice. Emotional turbulence. But if you pay them, the chances of a favorable outcome may be far higher

Anyone who has been a student-athlete knows the feeling heading into the summer before senior year. A hard realization hits you in the face: The end of collegiate sports is upon you. You start to reflect on the past three years and wonder what lies ahead.

For me, what lay ahead was another crucial turning point in my story...

I remember finishing up my spring finals and knowing it was summer. Everyone has heard the saying, "Live life to the fullest with no regrets." Very basic, I know. But for some reason, during that phase of my life, it was sticking. I found myself digging deeper into it, thinking about basketball. I knew I wasn't happy with what I was doing. I needed to make a change. It was time for me to take a risk...

I had only one year of eligibility left, and I wanted to finish my athletic career knowing I had given it everything I could. I wanted to leave the game I loved without any "what-ifs."

"When you are not in the conversation, you have to
make a *change*."
"When you are in the conversation, you just have to
make an *adjustment*."
— Kenny Smith

My first step was to register for summer school so I could participate in summer workouts with the team. Coaches made attending at least one summer session mandatory for scholarship players; for walk-ons, it was optional. I remember hearing scholarship players complain about having to work out during the summer. On my end, it was all I wanted to do.

The cost was over $1,200 a session for *one* class. I spoke with my parents and told them if I was ever going to be taken seriously by my coaches and have any opportunity to play minutes, then I had to participate in summer workouts. My parents always had been extremely supportive when it came to basketball, yet they hadn't seen my progression since I had almost never played in games. Nevertheless, they said if I truly believed it was important, then I should trust my instincts and do it.

During my first three years, I had focused my attention

on getting good grades and avoiding mistakes on the basketball court—the definition of "playing it safe." I was proud of the person I had become. I always tried to listen and do what was best for the team. But here's what's important: It took me three years to realize I had paid my dues in this role. I was ready for more. Participating in summer workouts would provide me an opportunity to compete in drills for the first time. I had to do it.

I paid the cost, enrolled in the first summer session, and never looked back.

In the regular season, 15 guys were fighting to get reps in practice; summer sessions cut that number in half. Since summer sessions were split in two, there were never enough players on campus at the same time. This lack of players gave a walk-on like myself a huge opportunity to compete. In summer workouts, I would no longer be an extra body on the sideline. I was actually needed on the court—a complete identity shift. There would be no uncertainty about whether I was allowed to hop into a drill. I could just play the game without any mental pressure.

So, once the summer session began, I was actually shooting in the shooting drills, not just rebounding. I was playing in the scrimmages, not watching from the sideline. I broke through the mental barrier that had built up all those years. Receiving this fair opportunity to compete and show my team what I could do as "Niksha Federico" was eye-opening.

During one of the first workouts, we were split into two

teams for a scrimmage. As crazy as this sounds, it was the first time in three years I was competing with some of my teammates. I'd always been playing against them, as a scout-team member. I was trying to keep calm, but deep down I was nervous playing in front of all the coaches. As long as I wasn't a liability, I figured that would equal success. As the scrimmage progressed, I gained a better feel for the pace of the game. I hit back-to-back 3s to end the workout. My confidence skyrocketed. For the first time, I truly started to believe I could sustain playing at this level.

Summer workouts were a grind. Physically, I had never been so tired, but mentally I had never felt fresher. Heading into one of the final workouts of summer, a staff member approached me when I was alone in the locker room. He sat down next to me and quietly asked, "Have you ever thought about redshirting?"

The thought had never crossed my mind. Why would it? I was just a walk-on who had seen a total of 30 minutes of official game time. The only people who had seen me play had done so during practice, and neither my coaches nor my teammates had ever mentioned anything about my game or my future. The last time my friends or family had seen me play was during high school, so they never said anything either. They were happy and proud whether I played or not. Personally, I had given up thinking about a future in basketball. I was just happy to finally participate in all the drills.

This staff member then told me my chances of realistically working my way into the rotation were low due to matters beyond my control but stressed that I had developed into a high-level player. He pointed out that, since I had only one year of eligibility remaining, this would be my last chance to have a decision over my basketball future. He finished by saying he was convinced that, with the right opportunity, I would be a game-changer for another program.

I was shocked he was even telling me this! I hesitated to answer him at first. I mean, this was the first time since high school I was having a conversation with somebody who believed in my game. I didn't know how to react. Even though he seemed confident, I was unsure. Being a late bloomer, I was anxious about going through the whole recruitment process again. But I was a completely different player than I had been in high school. Plus, I had grown three inches since then (up to 6'7"), and I had put on over 20 pounds of muscle. Maybe he was right?

I told him I would think it over and speak to my family.

Prior to that conversation, I had been directing most of my energy into taking pre-medical courses, attacking every day on the basketball court, and trying to have a positive impact on the program. The most I had envisioned for basketball was to be able to try and play heavy minutes as a senior with the added goal to play alongside my two roommates, who were also graduating at the same time. It was our last year together, and we wanted it to be special.

A month after the summer session ended, that coach's question was still stuck in my head. I didn't know what to do. I had many mixed emotions.

I mean, I had to wonder where I would even get a chance to play. The only game footage or highlights I had was knocking in a few 3s with a minute left in blowout wins. My stats were nothing. The other problem was, I already had made up my mind and planned out the next stage of my life, which at that time was following the path to medical school. The prospect of redshirting was really throwing a wrench in my med-school plans.

After long days of soul-searching, one thought inside me continually repeated itself: "What if?" I knew I loved the game of basketball, and I knew I loved competing. I hadn't experienced the feeling of being on the court and competing with a team since high school. This aspect, I recognized, was absent and unfulfilled. The idea of having regrets and what-ifs really frightened me.

Time stops for no one. I thought long and hard. What finally helped me come to a decision was imagining drinking coffee with my 45-year-old self. I asked him how he was doing, about the best decisions he had ever made, about his biggest regrets. Right off the bat, he said his greatest regret was never finding out how good he was at basketball. He regretted playing things too safe. He regretted not taking that leap of faith into the unknown.

There it was: I had my sign.

I knew if I didn't at least try to save my last year of eligibility and see if I had a chance to play, I would regret it for the rest of my life. Medical school wasn't going anywhere; one year, in the grand scheme of things, was nothing. So, one summer day in the backyard of my parents' house, I made up my mind.

I was going to redshirt.

CHAPTER EIGHT

"Acknowledge all of your small victories. They will eventually add up to something great."
— Kara Goucher

For me, the smallest possibility of receiving a scholarship from another school and continuing to play the game I love—not to mention seeing new things and meeting new people—trumped suiting up as a senior walk-on. Why not see what I was capable of? Sure, I would see a couple minutes during home-game blowouts; I would have my family on the court with me for Senior Night. Those were nice things. But I just wanted to *play*.

I figured, "I've already been paying my way for four years of classes…" The idea there was even a chance of a university paying for my school, giving me a monthly stipend, believing in me, and letting me play, was completely worth the risk.

I had put in four years of grueling practices, going hard against my teammates every day. Three of those years, our defense was considered top five nationally—so I knew my game had improved drastically from high school. It was time to see just how much…

I had made a firm decision but delayed telling anyone about it and making it official. I had trouble breaking free of the mental routine of seeing myself as a lowly walk-on. Don't be too hard on yourself.

I finally informed Coach Fisher of my plan to redshirt at the last official practice before our first game—in other words, on the very last day before I'd lose my eligibility.

Coach was indifferent about the decision. He just shrugged and said, "Okay."

As soon as I was officially redshirting a giant weight was lifted from my shoulders. For the first time, I was finally able to take a pause, finally able to breathe. All that pressure I had put on myself to change my situation had vanished. I was content.

My decision to redshirt had changed my identity on the team, both in my mind and from a public standpoint. I was no longer an eligible walk-on who was available to travel and play, but never did. I was now a redshirt senior who was unavailable to travel or play. There was no more uncertainty. I no longer had to worry about fielding those confused texts and calls from friends and family during away games. I now had a real answer. I finally had control of my situation, and having control allowed me to thrive.

For one, I no longer had to be emotionally invested in every situation during practice. It's not like I'd be suiting up for games. I could finally focus on having fun. And you know what? I started playing better basketball than I ever had before, reclaiming a calm confidence I hadn't felt since high school. Plus, as a redshirt I was no longer stuck in limbo when it came to team culture. I had established my own community within the team dynamic.

That season there were four redshirts: an extremely talented 6-10 freshman who was told to redshirt by the coaching staff, an all-conference transfer who was slotted as the starting point guard the following year, a preferred walk-on shooting guard who got injured and wanted to save a year, and me.

I had lucked out with these guys. We all complemented each other well and had great on-court chemistry. Our scout team, mostly redshirts, would often beat up on the starters during practice. We were a scary sight; competing with them was a blast. Off the court, we were all extremely close, too. When the team went on the road, the four of us would hang out, work out, and watch the games together.

Redshirting allowed me to work out far more than I had been able to do as an eligible walk-on. Since I wasn't suiting up for games, I didn't have to worry about resting during the hours leading up to home games. I could hit the weight room hard and then hit the court for a basketball workout. And that was our routine: We'd work out for around three hours before games, finish about 45 minutes before tip-off, then go support our teammates. It didn't matter if we were exhausted—all we had to do was sit on the bench and watch the game. Having a year of this routine afforded me with an amazing chance to focus strictly on improving myself rather than worrying what the coaches thought of me or whether I would be playing in games.

CHAPTER NINE

"The future rewards those who press on. I don't have time to feel sorry
for myself. I don't have time to complain. I'm going to press on."
— Barack Obama

Halfway through my redshirt year, my hard-work and micro
habits transformed into dominance. I was playing with a
sense of freedom and decisiveness that was hard to guard. I
felt in charge of my fate, in total control, and no one could
take that away from me. I was in flow. The next thing I knew,
Coach Fisher was pulling me aside, standing there telling me
he wanted me to play—that there was a huge opportunity
at my position. I couldn't believe what I was hearing! I had
dreamt of this moment for so long…

But the real situation turned out to be far trickier
than I could have even imagined.

Soon thereafter, I had just gotten out of class and
was heading to the arena for shootaround and the normal
game-day routine. Today was our conference game of
the year. The season so far had its ebbs and flows, but
it was looking like we were starting to head in the right
direction. I gave my customary head nod and fist bump to
the security guard at the entrance to the parking lot and

continued to the front doors of the arena. I was zoning out to Frank Sinatra, one of my go-to artists for long walks across campus.

Coach's car passed by me and parked in the spot closest to the door. I walked by him, smiled, gave a little wave, same as I had done every day for the past four years. But today was different—way different.

Instead of getting out like he normally does, Coach stayed inside the car and waved me over. He had never done that. I looked behind me…to my left…to my right… just to make sure he was signaling me and not someone else. I quickly paused "My Way," yanked out my headphones, and walked over. He waited for me to get closer before finally getting out. He stood right outside his door, keeping things private.

Coach began to tell me how happy he was with the way I had been playing in practice and how much value it had on preparing the team for games. Hearing this praise from an all-time great was an incredible feeling. Then, he said that he needed me to do him a favor. Surprised, I was like, "Sure, Coach. How can I help you?"

What he said next caught me off guard. He requested that I remove my redshirt and suit up for the remainder of the season… He articulated how beneficial it would be for the team—that there was a huge opportunity for my skill set on the court.

On one hand, I was elated. I mean, this was all I had

wanted for four years: to be seen. I long yearned for the opportunity to compete with these guys and help the team win, to validate all my hard work. And to get that from Coach Fisher—so highly respected, a true legend, the most celebrated coach in my school's history—felt amazing.

On the other hand, the team had already traveled to Hawaii and Vegas for tournaments without me. Half the season I had already missed. There were like 15 games left, and who really knew how much time I'd see?

I took a breath, then politely explained how I had been waiting four years for him to tell me this. I told him I was grateful for his consideration and the opportunity but reminded him that I couldn't really afford to suit up and lose my last year of eligibility this late in the season. The most important decision of my life began to weigh heavily over me!

Do I take the short-term gratification of finishing the season or delay the gratification and embrace the unknown of my untapped potential?

Coach started telling me there would be a jersey waiting for me in the locker before the game tonight when, out of nowhere, like a guardian angel, I heard someone yell, "What's up, Coach! What's up, Niksha!"

One of my teammates was walking into the arena, headphones on, strawberry smoothie in hand, no idea of the tension he'd just interrupted. We both waved. He made some sarcastic joke about the weather, laughed, then walked into the arena. Coach and I looked back at each other, trying to reassemble our conversation, but the intensity had evaporated. While my teammate was talking, I'd had time to take a breath and think. That brief time to reflect kept me from making an immediate decision based on emotion—one that would have huge repercussions on my future. I grabbed control of the dialogue, hoping to buy myself some more time.

"How about we talk about this more after shootaround?"

He looked at me and agreed.

I immediately put my headphones back on to show I was done talking. There was no music playing. We walked into the arena together. Coach went into the coaches' room; I went into the locker room. I silently dapped up all of my teammates and then proceeded to my locker like any normal game day, headphones still on, no music. I sat down, took a deep breath, and tried to process what the hell had just happened…

For Coach, bringing me back made total sense. To his credit, he was in a tough situation. The season was not going as we had intended, and I'm sure he was getting pressured by the media to pick things up and start winning some games. His job was to win. He knew I could help, so I don't really blame him for asking me to suit up that day. And it was humbling; it felt good that he believed in what I was capable of on the court. That moment was more than an opportunity;

it was confirmation that all my systematic habits and tweaks actually worked. But also, it meant that there was another level of untapped potential that I could possibly reach.

So in the end, the amazing offer was too late. It made no sense for me to choose the short-term gratification of finishing the season. The uncertainty of who I could become appealed more than the dim shadows of structured familiarity.

It was my decision, and I wasn't going to commit to anything based on a five-minute conversation in a parking lot.

As a walk-on, there will be situations where you need to say no, delay the instant gratification, and do what is in your best interest.

MAKE YOUR OWN DECISIONS—no matter the emotion or pressure of the moment.

CHAPTER TEN

"Be firm with your intentions, but flexible with your strategies for getting there. It pays to take risks and think outside the box. Nobody will do that for you, but you."
— Ronnie Fieg

After I had graduated, my name entered the transfer portal, and it all became real. I didn't know what to expect. So now what? What do I do?

As I mentioned, my résumé was razor thin. I knew a graduate walk-on with 30 total minutes of official court time in four years looked poor on paper. The only game footage I had was hitting back-to-back 3s in the final seconds of a blowout win in my freshman year and hitting another 3-pointer in the last minute of a blowout in my junior year. Three shots. Literally, that was it. I was scared no program would want me.

But I knew my numbers and in-game footage failed to depict the player I had become. I was bigger, stronger, and a completely different player by the time I had left San Diego State.

Luckily, most of the practices throughout the years had been recorded. I got the team's student managers to send me the practice films from my redshirt season. I figured coaches at the schools I'd be reaching out to would recognize the starters; if they could see me lighting them up, it would be a much better portrayal of what I could do than my stats. I needed all the credibility I could get. I watched every single minute and eventually decided it'd be best to compile my highlights into a video résumé.

One of my assistant coaches offered to help me get my name out to other programs. He respected my character and believed in the player I had become. He told me he would reach out to coaches and try to land me somewhere. However, no matter what he would say to other coaches, it always came down to the same things:

Well, why didn't he play for you guys then? There has to be something wrong with him. His ego? Attitude? Is he soft? Doesn't work hard? There has to be something you're not telling me...

Their skepticism was understandable, but I possessed none of these hidden flaws. It was simply a matter of timing and the great teams I had been fortunate to be part of. When I made the team as a walk-on, we were elite. Three of the four years I was in the program, we won a championship, which was an experience I'll never forget. I remember listening to a podcast during my freshman year and hearing someone say, "If the team is winning championships, who are you to complain about playing time? Get over yourself, enjoy the moment, and keep working hard." I have carried this principle with me throughout my basketball career. As long as we were winning, I could rest on that principle.

But now I was in a storm of uncertainty. A month had passed since graduation, and I still had received no serious interest or calls from any schools.

It's very important to have at least one person you trust, someone who has unwavering faith and confidence in you to help push through the fear of transitioning into the unknown. For me, this was my mom. She was the rock I could lean on whenever I was down.

I can clearly remember sitting with my mom at the kitchen table one hot summer day and her saying, "That's it! Time to take matters into our own hands. Enough waiting around." By then, it was already July. The transfer window was closing. I thought, "If you want something that bad, go out and get it!"

We began by creating a shortlist of schools across the nation I would love to attend. Then we went to each school's website, gathered the email addresses of every staff member (from the head coach all the way down to the graduate assistant), and sent all of them my highlight video. I included a personal introduction and details about my immediate eligibility for the upcoming season. The subject line was: "6'7" Graduate SG, SF Transfer Eligible to Play."

I laugh at this now, but when I was desperate, "sounding cool" went right out the window. I had no sense of entitlement. Zero care in the world. If I had to cold email programs, I was going to be *that guy*—and I was fine with that. We sent out 72 emails to a dozen universities (six staff members per program).

I received my first response literally 10 minutes after the last of the emails went out—from the assistant coach of a big-time university: "Hello, Niksha. Thanks for reaching out. Unfortunately, our team roster for the upcoming year is already full. Best of luck."

His reply could have seemed like a failure, but it was weird. I saw it as a major success. My mom looked at me and said, "We have to send your video out to more coaches." What had begun as my "Top 12" changed into a much larger list.

We started with where I would be open to living for nine months. California, my home state, was at the top, followed by places like Colorado, Hawaii, Massachusetts, Washington, and more. We then looked up every DI school in those states, found the basketball website for each, looked up the staff members and their email addresses, and sent all of them the same recruiting package. We had a great system. My mom was on her iPad researching schools; I would gather coaches' names and email addresses from the schools she found, modify the template, and send the emails from my laptop. I made sure to direct each email to specific coaches by name, hoping this would increase the likelihood of my message actually being read. In a few short hours, we were able to send out 600 tailored emails to different coaches across the country.

Many DI programs gave me looks, but it all came

down to, "You look really good in practice, but practice is not the same as playing in a game. You haven't played in a game in four years, so you're not going to be ready. We can't take the risk." Every time I got that response, it stung. Sure, I hadn't played a game in four years but how much different could that really be? If anything, I thought playing in a game would be easier. In games, there are actual refs who call fouls, actual fans who energize you. Seeing that response come up time and time again definitely motivated me even more to prove them all wrong.

Not one DI school offered me a full-ride scholarship, but some did offer preferred walk-on spots. I didn't want to go down that road again. I was looking for a fair chance to compete for playing time, and I was clear that another walk-on position would put me at a disadvantage. The only way I could get a real shot was with a scholarship. In college basketball, coaches can make all types of promises and share their visions of how you might fit in with their programs, but money talks. With only one year left of eligibility, I knew without a scholarship on the table, I would lack a truly fair opportunity to actually play.

In the end, over 200 schools either politely turned down, rejected, or didn't read my pitch. However, I received positive responses and serious interest from five universities who beforehand had no idea who I was. In my eyes, this was a huge win—in the span of 24 hours, I went from having zero universities interested to five being extremely interested.

Before my name entered the transfer portal, I was unaware that DII schools also offered full-ride scholarships that covered tuition, board, and even a monthly stipend. A lot of people underestimate the talent in DII, but there's always that random DII team with outstanding chemistry and experience who knocks off a powerhouse DI team in pre-conference play.

Among the DII programs that were interested, it came down to three schools for me. Two were in Hawaii: Chaminade University and Hawaii Pacific University. The third was a school in Boise, Idaho, which was definitely a different type of scene for my liking. I really liked the coach, though, and the fact that they showed me the most interest was something I found important. They were also offering me the best scholarship financially. However, I had been a beach boy my entire life, and I figured Hawaii would be the perfect place to live and explore for nine months. I mean, it's Hawaii! After speaking to my mom and pondering over the best decision, we both agreed I would be happiest experiencing Hawaiian culture. It was an opportunity I just couldn't overlook. I kindly declined the Boise offer. It was down to two.

The two Hawaii schools were rivals. I was unsure whether they were aware they were both trying to recruit me, but that was not my problem. I was just looking for an opportunity.

Chaminade showed more interest initially, so I was set on going there. I knew who they were having watched them play in the Maui Classic each year along with San Diego State. I went through the whole process with them: speaking to their coach on a daily basis, researching what the program could offer. They saw my potential, but ultimately told me I was their second option at my position and there was another guy they were trying to recruit ahead of me. The assistant coach then told me they had the best player in the league returning and that they were a bit skeptical when it came to what I could bring to the table. He was worried that I hadn't played an official game in four years. Once again, I was too much of a "risk." In the end, he told me that it was a waiting game—they'd want to see what their other recruit would decide before giving me an official offer.

Man, I couldn't believe this was happening again. I had no intention of being anyone's second choice. I didn't want to go to a program that only "half" wanted me there. I wanted to be sure I would have a fair chance to contribute. So, that was that.

Luckily, I had the perfect opportunity to prove him wrong by attending a school in the same league—and their biggest rival.

The assistant coach at Hawaii Pacific really liked me, but when I contacted them, it was late in the process and they had already built their team. All they had left was one half-scholarship that covered tuition and books but excluded housing and a stipend. I couldn't commit to that. I had to be able to survive. I had already redshirted my senior year and skipped out on senior night with my best friends for the chance to play without coming out of pocket. I was done paying to play basketball. Without the extra money, I was finished. Period.

Plus, since the coach couldn't technically offer me a full scholarship, it made me worry that I wouldn't receive a fair chance at playing time, which had been my experience as a walk-on. As much as the money meant, playing was really my top priority. I understood the power having a full scholarship had in guaranteeing that.

I made all of this clear to the coach. He said he understood and that he would try his best to see what he could do. A couple days later, he called and told me more money had been added to my scholarship, which would now cover housing but still lacked the stipend.

After some heavy thinking, everything became apparent to me. All the experiences I had endured as a walk-on had led to this moment. I had to make my own sacrifices. Even though I wasn't getting the dream offer of a full scholarship and a guaranteed starting position, I would be living and playing in one of the most beautiful places in the world. I had been training for four years to get the chance to play. If that meant I had to live frugally on an island, I was game.

Still, before I committed, I wanted to make sure that my partial scholarship wouldn't lower my chances of receiving a fair opportunity to compete for a major role on the team. This was the walk-on in me talking. The coach repeatedly told me not to think twice about it, and that had it been earlier in the recruiting process they would have certainly offered me a full scholarship. He stressed that the limited scholarship did not reflect how seriously they wanted me to play there. It was simply all they had left to offer.

The next day, I called the coach and told him I would accept their offer and join the program, but I had one condition: No one was to know I was on a lesser scholarship. He happily accepted. The moment had arrived. I would finally be able to see what I was capable of.

I was off to Hawaii.

CHAPTER ELEVEN

"And now that you don't have to be perfect, you can be good."
— John Steinbeck

Standing at the airport, saying goodbye to my family and friends, fear started to set in. I had never been to Hawaii. I had never visited the school. My whole reality changed as soon as I boarded the plane. I looked at the monitor, which showed the six-hour flight path from San Diego to Hawaii. Six hours? I full-blown thought Hawaii was like two hours away. I hadn't realized I was going to be that far away from home. I put my headphones on and prepared to leave my comfort zone.

I can still remember looking out the window while flying over Oahu for the first time. Nervous as I was, it looked beautiful.

A graduate assistant picked me up at the airport and escorted me to the school, where I'd meet my head coach, Darren Vorderbruegge, for the first time. I felt a bit weird about the meeting; we'd spoken only a couple times on the phone. I had mainly dealt with the assistant coach, who, as I would come to find out, had taken a new position in another program a week before my arrival. So, here I was about to show up at Coach V's office, barely knowing him, with nine-months worth of packed suitcases. Fortunately, we hit it off right away. He put winning first, and was all about discipline so we connected immediately there.

I was just grateful to have the opportunity to actually play. Being a scholarship player felt different from the start. My teammates knew me as "the transfer," and that's all. They didn't know my background, that I hadn't traveled to a single regular-season away game, that I'd played only 30 minutes in four years. In their eyes, I was that dude—the DI transfer. I had never been more excited about playing.

On the other hand, some of my new teammates were disappointed about not playing DI ball. Despite playing heavy minutes in DII, they just wanted to experience the highlights of being part of a DI team. I came to realize that athletes often want what they don't have, no matter how good their situations might be. Go figure. Less comparing, more gratitude is always the best approach in my mind.

Although I was full of uncertainties, I still had a *huge* chip on my shoulder. I held it close to my heart, but deep down it was driving me. I was hungrier and more determined than I'd ever been. I may have been on scholarship, but I still had the underdog mentality from my years as a walk-on. I had something to prove, and nothing was going to stop me.

My first practice at HPU was eye-opening. Being a walk-on had accustomed me to playing with an extremely small margin of error. Practice was much easier as a scholarship player. I didn't have to make every shot or play perfect all the time. If I messed up, a coach was there to encourage me. I quickly established myself as one of the stronger players. My past experiences were allowing me to thrive in my new setting. Moreover, I had a voice among the team. It was actually fun.

I had always thought playing in a game would be easier than practice, but the recruiting process had made one thing abundantly clear to me: The doubters were real. So, I wasn't sure how I'd actually do come game time. In all honestly, I didn't really have any high expectations for my season. My goal was just to give it my all and try to put my team in the best position to win. Simple as that.

About two weeks before our first game, we were all in the locker room after practice, and while I was taking off my shoes, I overhead my teammates saying the Pac-West Preseason All-Conference teams had been released. They started talking about the different players listed and how good those players were, like those guys were untouchable. I stayed quiet. I had never heard of any of those guys. I really didn't know anything about our conference. But hearing my teammates debate about opposing teams and players got me excited.

Of course, my name wasn't even mentioned as being considered for a preseason all-conference team. Hell, I doubted I was even in the preseason starting lineup for my team. Nobody outside of practice knew who I was. One thing was clear, though: I had been playing against a top DI defense every day for the past four years. My SDSU roommate had won a MWC Defensive Player of the Year award, and I had learned how to score on him. So, the hype surrounding players in my new league fazed me none whatsoever. It only motivated me more—I had targets now. I casually asked one of my teammates in the know to tell me when we would be playing against any of the guys on the list. That same day, I went home, printed out the preseason all-conference squads, and put the names up in my closet.

As we got closer to our first game, which would be in Alaska, I knew I was more than ready. Yet, all that outside chatter, all those doubters, still had a small place in my mind. Two days before we'd be flying up north, I grabbed some coffee with my roommate, Emil. He had quickly become one of my best friends on the team, and I looked after him like a little brother. Emil was from Sweden—this was his first time in the U.S. Before coming to HPU, he had played for the Swedish National Team. So, though he was a freshman in terms of eligibility, he had a veteran's experience.

While having our coffee, Emil asked me what my thoughts were on the upcoming season. Before I even had a chance to answer, he said, "You know, you're the best player in our league. You're going to be a pro. I can't wait to come see you play in Europe. We'll be close to each other."

I just took a sip and shook my head. I couldn't take him seriously.

Finally, we were in Alaska. Game Day. My first in four years. Though my nerves were tingling before tip-off, it wasn't close to the level of anxiety I had experienced sitting on the end of the bench as a walk-on. If anything, I was just anxious to see how I'd match up against the competition. The playing itself never really made me nervous. I had won the starting small-forward position, so I knew I was going to see real minutes—and that's all I needed to know. The rest was just playing basketball. Once the ref tossed the ball into the air, the nerves immediately vanished.

As soon as play began, I quickly realized my time as a walk-on had turned me into a player with intense attention to detail, a high IQ, an innate sense of hustle, and an unparalleled motor. Transferrable skills.

I was finally able to see the results of all my hard work. I dropped 18 points and grabbed 10 boards with a block and two steals in 33 minutes. Plus, we got the win. I'd played three more minutes in my first game then I did my entire four-year career as a walk-on. I couldn't help but smile walking back into the locker room. All the doubters and critics had been dead wrong.

The 18 points I scored my first game ended up being my season low for the first 13 games I played. My second game I finished with 22 points and 8 rebounds. Third game, 26 points and 7 rebounds. Fourth game, in 20 minutes, 25 points and 14 rebounds. In my fifth game, 26 points and 18 rebounds. Sixth game, 30 points and 11 rebounds. Seventh game, 28 points and 12 rebounds. Eighth game, 22 points and 9 rebounds.

Then came the ninth. The game I had drawn a circle around in my mind: Chaminade. Having turned me down for "better" players a couple months earlier, I wanted to show them what they'd passed up, and I did just that: 33 minutes played, 24 points, 11 rebounds, two steals, and a huge victory over our rival.

I go into detail on the numbers not to brag, but to show that my long-term belief in myself prevailed. I became the unknown guy who had taken the league by storm.

I finished the season leading my league in points per game and rebounds per game while being Top 10 nationwide in double-doubles. I earned All-Region First Team, All-Conference First Team, and Conference Newcomer of the Year awards. My university named me Male Athlete of the Year and Male Newcomer of the Year. To finally see some results and recognition for all my hard work felt amazing—I will never forget it.

Sometimes success happens to people who aren't necessarily looking for it. Did I encounter uneasy, uncertain moments throughout the entire process? Yes. Did I have to sacrifice receiving less to get an opportunity? Yes. Was it worth every second? Absolutely.

True growth comes after a large leap into the unknown, and taking that leap of faith was the hardest part of my entire process. It made me a completely different person—a stronger person. It can happen to you, too.

Trust your gut. Work hard in the dark. Always believe in yourself.

And don't be afraid to leap into that unknown…

CHAPTER TWELVE

"Always remember, the universe has a way of leading you to where you are supposed to be, at the moment you're supposed to be there."
— Manal Rostom

Emil had been right along…

When that season came to an end, I was no longer an unknown walk-on who nobody wanted. Sure, maybe I'd dreamed about becoming a pro-basketball player way back before I'd been a walk-on, but I'd never planned on it. So, when agents were suddenly contacting me regarding representation, I had to pinch myself. Offers were coming in from all over Europe.

That was the moment I knew all my hard work had come to fruition. That was the moment I had found the light, at the end of the bench.

Emil was the engine persuading me to go for it; he told me I had worked too hard to pass on the opportunity to play pro basketball. He knew who I was as a person and what my skills were on the court. He was convinced both would translate amazingly into the European game. Also, knowing I was crazy about coffee, Emil said I'd love the lifestyle: coffee, coffee, and more coffee. I'd never been to Europe, so having Emil as a firsthand resource sealed the deal. After the success I'd had moving to Hawaii, breaking out of my comfort zone, and diving face-first into uncertainty, I was confident I could do it again.

I was headed for Spain.

When I printed out the contract, it was all so surreal. I couldn't help but think back to my first year as a walk-on driving back watching that entire Sweet Sixteen game from the stands. I knew how much this moment meant to that young walk-on who had nearly lost all belief in himself. I knew how far I'd come to reach this point in my life's journey. I was proud of myself. Getting paid to play basketball was a dream come true. I put pen to paper and signed the dotted lines. I was officially a professional basketball player.

From paying to play, to getting paid to play—I had flipped the script.

Before leaving for Spain, I spoke with friends who had already been playing professionally for a couple years, guys who knew me when I was just that walk-on who wasn't allowed into drills. They understood how much it meant to have gone from walk-on to pro, and I got an extra boost of confidence hearing they were proud of me, too.

My rookie year was a whirlwind, but I loved that it was a complete restart for every rookie who had made it to this point. I had broken through a paradigm. My teammates were no longer scholarship players—they were professionals. College politics were a thing of the past. Nobody cared about what you had or hadn't done in college. Nobody cared who you were. Nobody cared about your feelings. Each player had persevered to make it to this level, and on the court each player was an employee—all that mattered was whether you would be able to perform at a high level in the present moment. It was cutthroat. The pressure was immense.

I *loved* it.

I had arrived in Spain filled with momentum from my success in Hawaii and was ready to work. I was eager to start competing with my new team. My history of being a walk-on might have been behind me, but my walk-on mentality never wavered. The chip on my shoulder had only gotten bigger. Now, I had another chance to prove doubters wrong. Now was my real opportunity. I would be competing against the guys I used to watch from the end of the bench or on TV.

The first year as a pro is all about establishing credibility. You have to prove yourself every day. For players used to having a long leash as a star in college, it ain't sweet anymore. Again, European coaches don't care what you did, only what you can do. This worked in my favor—I had already experienced the bottom rungs. I had already built in the habits to face adversity and knew how important proving yourself from the jump could be to your trajectory.

So, I treated my rookie year as if I were a walk-on all over again. My actions in practice were exactly the same as the player who had sat at the end of the bench all those years. I focused all my attention on doing the little things.

I tried to be the first guy in the gym and the last to leave. I consistently went the extra mile for my teammates and staff. I built a strong relationship with my coach, routinely asking his opinion on how I could improve. I was trying to learn something new every day. No matter how much better the situation was, I attacked every day with a walk-on's mindset. I was stepping in a professional's shoes, but I was still a walk-on at heart. The reality was, I was no longer at the end of the bench.

Training camp was a *grind*. We had two or three practices a day, seven days a week. There were 12 players on payroll and five starting spots. You can only imagine what the intensity levels were like those first couple months before games began. I had never played that much basketball in my life. It's not like I had any homework to do for school anymore; all of my focus was on basketball. Making the jump from college to pro definitely took some time to adjust. The overall pace was faster; there was more strategy involved; the physicality was on a whole different level. Players were bigger, stronger, more athletic. I understood I could no longer be Niksha Federico from Hawaii. I had to adapt my game. This meant not only changing how I played and the types of shots I took, but who I was both on and off the court. Certain moves and shots of mine that worked in college were simply no longer efficient at the pro level. I can't tell you how important breaking down and dissecting my game was in allowing me to continue to beat out my competition on the court.

I believe playing thousands of hours of different styles each week on the scout team had subconsciously made it easier for me to alter my game more than others. My goal was to position myself to play with a role that could bring immediate winning value to any pro team at any level. I wanted my game to be as specific and efficient as possible, while simultaneously being positionless. It took some time, but eventually I figured it out. It is called your rookie season for a reason.

Coming out of training camp, I had passed the first test as a pro and managed to establish myself as the starting small forward. I was exactly where I needed to be. As much as being a walk-on was full of adversity, it equipped me with the invaluable skill of adaptability.

Once games began, though, I quickly discovered the true differences between being a student-athlete and a pro player. Players aren't lying when they say your sport becomes a full-time job once you turn professional. The game was no longer something I just played; it was a business. If we won, the club was happy, and everything was amazing. If we lost, it was as if the world was coming to an end. The higher ups in the club made it clear: Players on contract were there to work hard, perform, and win games. But the club's owner had never played basketball before, so he didn't understand that all of that can be a process.

The general manager and my coach had compiled a team full of rookies with the aim of playing at the fastest pace possible. The Spanish league generally is known for having a slower, skilled, methodical game. The best teams in the league had rosters of experienced, smart, gritty, talented basketball players who knew how to win. They weren't always fancy in how they won, but damn those teams were tough to beat.

This quickly taught me the importance of winning as a professional and how being in a winning environment was crucial for progression. I had spent my entire basketball career on winning teams, so I had never experienced being a part of a losing culture. That made my rookie year stressful, but I learned the small finite line between winning and losing at the professional level.

I was still shocked that I was being paid to play the game I loved, finding extra motivation to play hard was getting easier than ever.

CHAPTER THIRTEEN

"Sometimes life brings you full circle to a place you have been before,
just to show you how much you have grown."
— Unknown

Scrolling through Twitter during lunch one day, I noticed that the Cáceres team account was blowing up. Apparently, they had just signed a new player as a late addition to their roster. The tweet read, "Bienvenidos Angelo Chol!" No way. I couldn't believe it. I looked at the picture and, sure enough, there was one of my best friends. I texted him to make sure it was real. He said he was indeed on his way to Spain, and he'd be living about three-hours' drive from me.

Angelo was a big-time player at San Diego State, but he always had my back—something for which I'll always be grateful. He was two years older than me, but we got really close my first year. He was like a big brother to me, always including me in everything and treating me the same as anyone else, scholarship or not. We even ended up living as roommates for a year. This was my guy.

Who could have imagined back during that Sweet Sixteen game that we'd be facing each other as professionals in Europe? I was so excited to see him, especially this far away from home. He'd always known me as a walk-on. I couldn't wait to play his team and see what he would think now.

Our team was in a funk leading up to that game. We were on a losing streak and dealing with adversity within the club. I was having a great year individually, but the team not so much. It definitely got frustrating at times; when we'd lose, I was incredibly hard on myself. I've always judged the way I played on whether my team won or lost the game—never my own stats—so I was having a hard time.

On game day, we arrived at 10:00 a.m. for our scheduled shootaround, which always took place seven or eight hours before tip-off. Players use that time to feel out the arena, get some shots up, and stretch out a bit. Coaches use that window as a chance to make last-minute adjustments to game plans. The away team would always get an hour on the court before the home team would take over. Strategically speaking, this scheduling gave the home team the advantage since the visiting team would get less sleep before the game. It also prohibited the opposing team from getting extra time on the court. Front offices look for any advantage to give their teams higher chances to win, even if it's as small as preventing one more shot on the court before the game. Things could definitely get petty at times, such as when home teams would send passive-aggressive signals like walking onto the court the exact second the hour ended.

Of course, there were always worries that home teams would be spying during visiting teams' shootarounds.

Depending on the location, our staff members would be tasked with making sure scouts weren't lurking in the shadows. It was always funny to see the coaching staff stressing about espionage; they made sure nothing too revealing would take place during our hour.

Normally, though, when the two teams were transitioning, that gave personnel a chance to cross paths and catch up in a civil manner. Spanish players loved interacting with members from opposing teams. The local veterans all knew each other, and it was common to see players hugging and chatting.

Being my first year, I didn't know any of the guys I was playing against. When shootarounds ended, I'd put on my headphones, deliberately avoiding eye contact with the opposition as I packed up my stuff and headed for the bus. I never liked talking to opposing teams before games—I always felt like that would give me less of an edge. Chatting after a game was one thing, but never before. That's just me.

However, for this shootaround, I was completely different. I'd been living across the world for five months, and I was a little homesick. I could care less about having an edge. Angelo was my brother, and I wanted to see him. When my team's hour ended, I drained one last deep 3-pointer and then went to the bench. I untied my shoes slowly, hoping I'd get a chance to see Angelo. As more and more players trickled in, he was still nowhere to be found. I couldn't wait much longer. Disappointed, I put on my headphones and began to walk away. As I was taking my last step off the court, I heard a loud, "FEDERRRICOOO!" I looked back and saw him coming out of the locker room. "ANGELOOO!"

It was a special moment. We gave each other a big hug. We had always kept up over texts, but finally seeing each other in person after spending all those years together was different. He said that my profile had come up a few moments earlier when his coaches were delivering the scouting report. He couldn't believe what I had accomplished and that he had a huge smile on his face each time he saw my highlights. He knew I was killing it. We kept it brief, said our goodbyes, and agreed to meet up after the game. I no longer felt homesick.

Game time. The arena was filling up. Even before the game, fans were already playing drums, singing, chanting. Cáceres had a solid fan base. The atmosphere was electric.

The European atmosphere was much different than in college. European fans would come with large flags, drums, horns—constantly playing music, heckling, singing chants they had composed for their team. From the opening tip to the final buzzer, you could feel the love and passion these fans had for their clubs and for the sport of basketball. It was real.

I had a feeling the game was going to be a great one, but I treated the game like any other. I went through my normal starter's routine: I'd doff my warmups, tuck in my jersey, and then I'd give everyone—from the team doctor at the end of the bench to my teammates in the middle and then the coaching staff and my head coach—a high five and a hug, saying, "Let's do this! Good luck!" Having that routine triggered a state of concentration and locked me in for competition. Once I was on the court, I would then shake hands with all the refs and opposing players before taking my position for tip-off, ready to go.

Every game has a few seconds of pure anticipation before the ref blows the whistle and tosses the ball up in the air. I've always been intrigued by this brief window. What is every player thinking? Are they even thinking? I've always tried to regulate my breathing and calm myself while making eye contact with teammates to boost their confidence.

For this game, though, rather than focusing on my breath I found myself glancing over to the other team's bench. And there was Angelo, staring right back at me. He was on the bench. I was on the court. In just three years, our roles had completely reversed. Wild.

In that brief moment, I was able to pause and see my situation from a greater perspective. Yes, my team was on a losing streak, but that shouldn't cloud my happiness over how far I'd come and where I was in the present. Less than 18 months earlier, I was praying for a few minutes of court time at SDSU. Now I was a starter playing 30 minutes per game as a professional. Win or lose, I had succeeded. My goals had become my reality. I couldn't let the pressure of my club overwhelm that.

I came out hot, tipping in an offensive rebound for my

team's first bucket and then hitting back-to-back 3s. I was having fun again. Instead of allowing the club's adversity to weigh on me, I focused on basking in the moment and play the game I loved.

Angelo finally checked in with about four minutes left in the first quarter. I couldn't help but grin. Here we were, sharing the same court halfway across the world in front of thousands of fans—pretty different from doing workouts in a dark, empty gym back on campus. It was a cool moment.

When our team had been going over the scouting report, I told my coach Angelo was much stronger than they had assessed. I left thinking the matchup Coach had planned for Angelo was going to be trouble for us. I was right. Angelo scored six quick points as soon as he entered, completely dominating my teammate in the post. The first quarter ended with Angelo getting a tip-in at the buzzer. The home crowd went crazy. He had singlehandedly shifted the game's momentum.

That energy continued into the second quarter. Cáceres went on an 8–0 run behind back-to-back 3s and a wide-open dunk by their big man. The entire arena went into a frenzy. Rather than take a timeout, Coach signaled us to keep playing. I in-bounded the ball to our point guard from beneath our basket. He called for a quick ball screen, but lost his footing, slipped, and lost the ball. Our shooting guard dove for the ball, but ended up knocking it directly into the hands of an opposing player. The crowd let out an even louder roar.

Since I was the in-bounder, I was the only player back on defense facing what quickly became a two-on-one fast break. In my head, I knew we needed to quiet the home crowd somehow. I waited for one guy to commit to the rack, then I fouled him. *Hard*. It was a smart foul. I couldn't let him make the shot and give his team and the crowd that much more momentum. When I hit his arm, though, his own momentum sent him flying onto the ground, making the foul look much worse than it was. My bad…

Things escalated from there. The crowd turned ugly; the entire arena of Spanish fans had their arms in the air, pointing at me, cursing me. The player I fouled sprung off the ground and angrily sprinted at me, getting in my face. He shoved me and kept talking trash as he got closer. He started squaring me up like he wanted to fight. I stayed calm—time slowed way down.

Then, out of nowhere came Angelo, like a guardian angel. He shoved his own teammate away from me and got between us. I could hear him yelling, "He's good! He's good! Relax, he's cool!" The impending brawl fizzled. The player eventually gathered himself and went to shoot his free throws. The crowd was still screaming at me, but the on-court tension was done. Here we were, competing against each other in Spain, yet when it really came down to it, Angelo still had my back…

The entire game was hard-fought, but Angelo's team ended up with the victory. As the final seconds ticked off the clock, all the players began shaking hands. The player who had tried to fight me came up and apologized. He told me the energy in the arena had got the best of him and he didn't realize who I was.

Who I was?

Soon thereafter, Angelo would tell me the guy was his current roommate. I laughed so hard upon hearing that. I mean, was the guy trying to fight me over the foul or because I was the cooler roommate? I choose to believe the latter.

After my coach's post-game speech, Angelo and I met on an empty court. Before I could say anything, he said, "Bro, I am so proud of you. Seeing you out there playing at this level made me so happy. If I ever have a son, I want him to be like you when he grows up—to never give up."

It was one of the nicest things anyone had ever said to me. And it meant even more coming from him.

CHAPTER FOURTEEN

"Every adversity creates a seed for a greater road."
— Napoleon Hill

After Christmas, everything seemed to go downhill. I fell on my wrist and finished the season on the injured-reserve list. My club fired our head coach in the second half, then the team fell apart under the new head coach, losing the final nine games and finishing in last place. Fortunately, my numbers carried real value, and I'd established myself as one of the top rookies in the league. At the very least, I'd proven I could match the level of competition, positioning myself to get into a new situation with a better club.

Though I'd accomplished my dream of playing professional basketball, I felt I had more to prove given the way the season had ended. I couldn't help comparing my rookie year to my first year as a walk-on—never really feeling connected to the team. In many ways, I was still searching for fulfillment on the court.

I came back to California that summer more physically and mentally exhausted than ever. I didn't want anything to do with basketball, didn't want to play basketball, didn't want to think of basketball. Mind and body, I needed a break; I took off the entire first month. It took all the energy I had left just to keep my hands off a ball, but I knew how important it was to rest, finally. From the day I'd arrived in Hawaii, I'd been playing and traveling nonstop. I needed to take a pause and reflect on the past two years. I needed to refresh my perspective, to regather my focus, to make new goals and attack them with a new mindset. That month off helped me find gratitude for the past and hope for the future.

What else did I really want? After digging deeper, I knew what was still missing. I wanted to be part of a winning team—more than that, I wanted to have a vital role on that team. I'd gotten all the playing time I could ever want— almost 35 minutes per game for two straight years. Now I wanted to win and play an important role in a team's success.

I started receiving offers from teams all over my league and in other parts of Europe. I soon learned that I'd certainly positioned myself in a better spot from a financial perspective, and many of the teams interested were winners. Now it was all up to me. I was in control. So, what did I want? I kept coming back to my search for true connection. Although I'd picked up the individual accolades, I'd still never felt as if I belonged. That's what I wanted.

So, would I go with the team that offered the most money or one that had established a winning culture? I wanted respect. Though I had done well my rookie year, there was still an asterisk after my name. I decided I needed to return to the same league but with a club that would allow me to thrive in a winning culture. Time would tell.

I finally had a bit of money saved up, so I decided to search for a personal trainer once my month of rest came to an end. All those summers as a walk-on, I'd conducted my own disciplined workouts, but this was my career now. I needed to build the proper team and resources around me. As a pro, I'd learned the importance of investing in yourself. If I wanted to make a real jump in my game, hiring a trainer was almost mandatory.

After interviewing several potential trainers, I decided to go with Trent Suzuki. His training style was different than all the other trainers I interviewed. He was old school, hard-nosed, hated excuses, spoke only about results. He didn't care about appearances, social media, or the newest weight-room trends. Plus, he had the credibility of producing real advancement for his clients.

Trent and I sat down together and outlined my goals for the summer and a game plan for how to achieve them. I presented a list of specifics on what I needed to improve for the following season. First, and most importantly, I needed to get my shooting wrist back to full strength as I still hadn't fully recovered. Secondly, I needed to focus on building core and lower-body strength—something that had hindered me during my rookie season. Lastly, I needed to put on as much muscle as possible. I was playing against men now, and it was almost impossible to sustain my weight over the long season. Muscle mass would be imperative in allowing me to succeed in my second year.

We set our target date to coincide with a client-only event being hosted by my agent in Las Vegas. I'd have a chance to play in front of scouts, general managers, and club owners from all over the world. It was a huge opportunity. I wanted to be healthy and fully recovered by then.

We had six weeks.

From Day One, Trent and I connected. He knew my story—knew the chip I had on my shoulder—and that helped us work well together. "Grind all summer, shine all winter" was his motto. He pushed me to levels in the weight room I never could have reached on my own. I gained 12 pounds of muscle. The only issue was, to make sure my wrist would fully recover, I'd been playing very little basketball.

If I had learned anything from my experience with open tryouts and exposure events, it was how crucial sustained confidence in yourself was to succeeding. I was healthier than ever, but I wasn't ready on the court. It just didn't feel right.

Pay attention to your gut. No matter how good something looks, if it doesn't feel right, walk away.

I had put up solid numbers as a rookie. The last thing I wanted to do was attend the event and completely drop the ball in front of everyone. After some heavy thinking, I decided not to play. Still, I was aware of the great opportunity the event provided me. Just being there could raise my stock by allowing scouts and executives to get a feel of who I was off the court. I called my agent and told him I'd be buying my own flight to Vegas. In my eyes, it was a win-win situation. Since I wouldn't have to worry about performing on the court, I could relax. I'd have the chance to network and discuss plans for the upcoming season with my agent face to face—something I needed to take advantage of as he was always in Europe.

When I arrived at the event, I sat with my agent in the bleachers alongside owners, GMs, and scouts. Some of them were in town to watch the NBA Summer League as well. Not playing gave me one-on-one access to my agent, who began telling me about all the teams he'd been talking to—one in particular, CBC Valladolid, was very interested. He thought it could be a great situation for me. They'd just hired a new head coach—Hugo Lopez—who would be returning to his hometown after several years coaching around the world. Lopez had previously been an assistant coach at Real Madrid and was the current head coach of the Swedish Men's National Team. My agent told me Lopez really liked my game and wanted to hop on a quick phone call. Two minutes later, I got a call from Coach Lopez.

I walked outside to answer. We spoke on the phone for a solid 20 minutes. He reaffirmed how much he liked my game and described what he was trying to build at his new club. He detailed the players who would be returning as well as the new players he was trying to bring aboard to jumpstart the program. I loved everything he was saying. We had similar views on what it takes to build a successful team. I could hear in his voice how badly he wanted to win. He wanted to bring something special back to his hometown. It was exciting.

I had played against CBC Valladolid as a rookie. They had a great home arena and a diehard fan base, which gave them one of the best home-court advantages in the entire league. They had finished in the top eight of 18 teams, reaching the playoffs, which would be a major step up from my rookie year. Coach Lopez had clearly been hired to take them to the next level. Valladolid didn't have the most money on the table, but I could tell the organization had a proud team culture.

The team was led by legendary Spanish veteran Sergio De La Fuente, who was universally respected throughout the league. The two times we had played them, he killed us. He was a power forward who consistently played dirty, but the league's refs respected him. He was also a great passer from the "4" position, something I knew would complement my game wonderfully. After being on the other side of that, I really wanted to play alongside him.

Coach Lopez said he saw me as the starting small forward, but he wanted to make sure my wrist was healthy before he committed. He was a bit skeptical because I wasn't playing in the Vegas event. I told him I wasn't playing so I'd be fully ready for the upcoming season and I wasn't worried whatsoever because I was in the best shape of my life. After the call ended, I went back into the gym. My agent was speaking with an owner. Eventually, he came back and sat down with me, curious to see how the call had gone. I told him I liked Coach Lopez and the call had gone well. We agreed to wait for an offer to decide how serious I was about them. It was still early.

While we were watching his clients scrimmage, one player kept grabbing my attention. He was a character to say the least—the guy talked without end to every person on the court, getting all of them laughing. I could feel the impact of his personality from the bleachers. The dude seemed hilarious. It might have seemed like he wasn't serious from all the joking and chatting, but I could tell it was his way of locking in. He was yelling on defense, slapping players' butts, making hustle plays look fun. He was killing it, too, making almost every shot he took, and he played with high basketball IQ. His team won every drill.

When I asked my agent who he was, he said, "Kimbal Mackenzie. Funny that you ask. Valladolid is very interested in him as well. They actually offered him last week."

Kimbal was a confident-shooting combo guard—a luxury for any team. Having just got off the phone with Valladolid, I knew I had to talk with him.

During a short break between scrimmages, Kimbal was alone grabbing a quick drink. I saw this as the perfect chance to approach him. We chatted for a while. Initially, he thought I was an agent since I had been sitting in the stands the entire time. I told him I had actually just finished speaking with Coach Lopez. Kimbal laughed and told me that he had grabbed a coffee with Lopez in Toronto a week earlier and said he was a really good dude. He also told me Lopez was known for being intense, but that he won championships—all super valuable information.

However, Valladolid was offering only shared apartments—a dealbreaker for him. He wasn't interested in living with someone that he didn't know; he wanted to move to Europe with his girlfriend. Fair enough.

I told Kimbal I had played against Valladolid as a rookie, and I had heard nothing but good things. Most importantly, I told him their captain, Sergio De La Fuente, gave Valladolid political power on the court—something my team of rookies lacked. The chance to play alongside Sergio was hard to overlook.

When we parted, I joked, "Hey man, who knows…? Possible roomies?"

He laughed and said, "See ya, roomie!"

I signed with Valladolid a month later. Kimbal saw the news and texted to congratulate me. Two weeks after that, Kimbal signed as well.

I'll give you one guess who my roommate was…

CHAPTER FIFTEEN

"You have to expect things of yourself before you can do them."
— Michael Jordan

From the moment we all arrived in Valladolid, everything clicked. Our team had the perfect balance of personalities—an equal number of players who spoke Spanish or English with several players who spoke both. The mix helped us develop a seamless communication that led to an amazing locker-room culture wherein we were all comfortably just being ourselves. It was beautiful—we were a team.

Everyone at Valladolid had their own underdog story. A consistent theme ran through the entire organization that gave everything an effortless chemistry. People felt as if they had been overlooked at one point or another—that Valladolid was a team being overlooked—so a spirit of perseverance was present from top to bottom. We had an indescribable energy. From the Club President to our GM to Coach Lopez to the last player on the bench, we were all hungry. We all had something to prove. We all wanted to win. I felt like I could contribute to that, that I belonged here.

After one week of practice, I was convinced we were the best team in the league. We hadn't even played a game together as a team yet, but I just knew. My eyes were set on winning a championship. Kimbal was only a rookie, but he felt it, too. We'd both been on championship teams during college. You can't really put a name to what that feeling is, but we definitely felt that same energy with Valladolid. Now we had to try to make the rest of the team believe that as well.

Training camp was intense. Coach Lopez set the bar extremely high from Day One. He left no margin of error for any player. He'd purposely set expectations that were almost impossible to maintain. He knew what he was doing: creating a standard of excellence that led to pristine, consistent basketball. He was molding us into high level professional players.

Coach Lopez had a charismatic swag that was fun to be around. At times he was definitely crazy, but I could always see the reasons behind his actions. I had never been around a coach that struck such a perfect balance between being extremely hard on his players while making sure every player knew he had their backs. He had it down to an art. He implemented a strict system, but he made us feel comfortable playing as ourselves and encouraged swagger.

The mutual respect between Coach Lopez and me was real. He recognized how serious I was about winning, and I understood how badly he wanted to win, too. He had a vision in line with my goals. To this day, I am grateful for the incredible transparency we were able to establish in our relationship.

I finally had that identity I had been longing for, and

I was proud of where I was. I was no longer sitting at the far end of the bench, watching others play every game. Nor would I be exhausted every night from having to carry an entire team's responsibilities on my back alone. I had established myself as the starting small forward on a championship contender. My team needed me to play as hard as I could and as efficiently as possible for 25 minutes per game. I knew what my team needed me to do, and I knew what I needed to do.

I introduced you to Emil back in Chapter 11. Unfortunately, an unexpected tragedy occurred. He collapsed after getting hit going for a layup in a game the previous year. A few days later, he passed away. As painful as the situation was, I always felt Emil with me on the court. It was he who drove me to play professionally. Days after I had officially signed with Valladolid, I spoke to the GM about how important it was for me to wear No. 10, which was Emil's number. I had worn No. 33 all my life, but I wanted to pay tribute to Emil. He was such a positive light for me, and I wanted to devote my season to him. A week later I received a text from the GM that made me smile: "#10 is all yours."

Our first preseason game of the season was against Palencia, our rival. It would be the first time suiting up as No. 10. When I went into the locker room and saw the jersey waiting for me, I got chills. I couldn't help but stare and smile. I put on my jersey and immediately felt Emil there with me, looking out for me, supporting me. He'd always had my back (and now was literally on my back). We won that game; I scored exactly 10 points, one rebound short of a double-double to make it 10 and 10. He wanted to keep me humble. Classic Emil. Not a day has gone by that I haven't thought of him and missed him.

Wearing No. 10 throughout the year allowed me to have true gratitude toward being able to play the game I loved. Even when I wasn't playing my best, rather than beating myself up I'd look at the number on my shorts, think about what Emil would want me to do, and refocus my energy on being grateful in the present moment. It was special.

We had a great preseason. After upsetting our rival, we went on to beat another well-respected team by 20. We were dominating teams and flowing really well as a unit. Our team had every aspect necessary for success on the court. We all complemented each other's games perfectly. It was almost reaching the point where things were clicking so well that we were tired of wasting it playing pre-season games, which meant nothing. We were anxious to get the real season going.

After an eye-opening preseason full of wins, it was time for the true test—to see if our team would be able to bring it all together. Building off that momentum, we never looked back. We started out by strongly winning our first few tests and then followed with a major winning streak to position ourselves atop the entire league.

The crazy thing was our club had the third-lowest budget of 18 teams. Yet, there we were singlehandedly defeating the teams with the highest payrolls. I guess that's what happens when you manage to fill a locker room full of players who have been overlooked their entire careers.

We had established ourselves in our club's history books, starting out with the best overall record to a regular season. More and more people began to believe. We were taking it day by day—that was the answer to every interview, question, or postgame analysis when asked whether we thought we were capable of winning the entire league. There was still a lot of basketball to be played, but deep down we felt we could continue building on our momentum.

The biggest game of the year was upon us. We were scheduled to play Breogán, the largest club in our league, at home. This club had a budget four times higher than ours, and they were in second place, only one game behind us. Breogán was the epitome of collecting as many "star" players as they could and paying them all enough to be on the same team together. Each player had promised careers and tons of hype surrounding him.

Neither the public nor the media thought we stood a chance. Meanwhile, the energy in our locker room before the game was calm and confident. We knew we could beat them. We knew we could prove everyone wrong. It was almost as every person in that locker room had been working years for an opportunity like this.

So, when they came onto our home court and the whistle blew, we came out with a vengeance. We set the tone from tip-off. The game was a hard-fought battle for four quarters, but we pulled it out in the end. It was the biggest win in our club's history and proved to the entire league that, no matter our budget, we were a team to be taken seriously. There was no longer any debate about if our team should be at the top.

Having our fans by our side allowed us to thrive all season. We knew we were playing for something bigger than ourselves. We had an entire city on our shoulders now. The noise we were making as underdogs, sustaining first place game after game, led to more and more support. We were the definition of a Cinderella story, and people wanted to be a part of what we were doing. The best thing about it was the manner in which we were beating teams—by playing efficient team basketball. It was beautiful to watch. Each player was embracing their role and making positive contributions.

The winning was benefiting our club as well. Things were quickly changing before our eyes. More sponsors began to appear; gym areas began to get refurbished; the locker room received major upgrades. Optimism was flowing throughout the entire organization.

Personally, I felt good. I was fresh in games. I wasn't completely exhausted as I had been in Hawaii and in my rookie year. My body was feeling great. I was consistently reaching a state of peak performance. So, not only was my team in first place, I was playing the best basketball of my career from an individual standpoint as well, leading the league in total efficiency rating while shooting over 50 percent overall, over 50 percent from 3-point land, and over 90 percent at the free throw line. I was on pace to finish out the season with every shooter's dream—becoming part of the 50–50–90 club. Plus, I was having more fun playing basketball than ever before.

We were in the top spot at the turn of the year. With two-thirds of the season completed, our success was no longer being questioned. We had held first place for 18 of the first 21 weeks. Then winning fatigue started to set in. Earlier in the season, we were underdogs gunning for top clubs. Now we were the team everyone was putting in their crosshairs. Sustaining the top spot got more and more stressful as the gravity of our situation increased. We were exhausted.

Here we were: a team full of players with the third-lowest payroll in the league with a chance to make the jump into the Liga ACB, the second-best league in the world behind the NBA. It would be an unparalleled ascension for every player in our locker room. A career-making climb. We all knew it, but never spoke about it. The real difficulty being at the top was searching for a new chip to put on our shoulders. We no longer had to worry about proving the doubters wrong. Our identity had completely flipped. None of us had ever experienced these new expectations. It was a new side of our sport.

Maintaining our spot began to take its toll, and adversity began to hit us from every direction. The pressure overwhelmed our entire organization. Often, it's better to be the underdog, to hunt rather than be hunted. We learned the difference very quickly.

Troubles came personally as well. I suffered a major sickness that kept me bedridden for a week and a half, losing five pounds of muscle, and missed an important road game that we ended up dropping in overtime. My first game back, I was still fighting fatigue and shot 0–8 from the field, but luckily, we still managed to win. Before I got sick, I would shoot with the expectation to make everything; I'd be shocked if I missed. After getting sick and having a couple rough games, I started shooting not to miss—a subconscious change that had a negative impact on my shooting confidence.

It's important to be aware of negative emotions, write them down, realize that they're just feelings, and move on to the next day. I thought about that 18-year-old walk-on who had simply hoped he would be able to participate in more than one drill during practice. In just my second year as a pro, I was the starting small forward on the league's best team fighting for a championship. I realized I had made it this far due to my mindset, confidence, and determination. Shooters shoot. A 0–8 shooting night only means one thing: The next eight shots are going in. I was not going to let one game dictate my journey.

With only a few games remaining before we could officially clinch the league title, celebrate the spoils of being champions, and make the leap into the Liga ACB, something beyond anyone's control occurred—something way bigger than basketball. Nothing could prepare us for what lay ahead. All the hard work, dedication, and grit we'd put into every single day since arriving in Valladolid eight months prior was about to be upended. We couldn't stop it, and nobody was ready…

CHAPTER SIXTEEN

*"Champions do not become champions when they win the event,
but in the hours, months, and years they spend preparing for it. The
victorious performance itself is merely the demonstration of their
championship character."*
— Alan Armstrong

I remember sitting at a local coffee shop I would go to on my days off to read and relax. The Spanish daily news channel was playing on a television. An anchor was reporting breaking news of an extremely contagious pneumonia-like virus spreading rapidly throughout mainland China. I drank my coffee, grasped by the report. Soon enough, though, the news switched to soccer highlights. That's Spain for you. I tried to refocus on my book, but two older men began arguing at a nearby table, debating the severity of what they called a "Chinese plague" and what it might mean for the rest of the world.

One of them was arguing that it wasn't a big deal. The other believed it would soon take over the world; he downed the last of his beer and said, "Think about how many people travel in and out of China. The virus could be here as we speak."

This could be bad…

Only hours after returning to my apartment, I'd find out that second gentleman was right. The first case of COVID was reported in Italy. The next 72 hours were shocking.

It was Tuesday. An intense practice was coming to an end. We had just come off a loss in our previous game and had been dealing with tons of built-up adversity from the previous weeks with players being injured or sick. It created a vast amount of tension between the front office, coach, and players. An important team meeting was held after practice to get us all back on the same page. The meeting served mainly as a safe space for players to speak their minds in a transparent manner over the miscommunication that was occurring on the court. We talked about the negative energy that had become present during games, about the building pressure, about getting back to how we had played in the beginning, and, most importantly, about how to overcome these trials and finish the last couple games strong so we could secure a championship. It was a powerful conversation. We were all confident we'd be able to get the ball rolling again.

Little did we know we would never play another game together as a team.

That next game was scheduled to be played at home on March 13, 2020, but in a matter of hours everything changed. Our captain sent a text to our group chat saying there were rumors coming from other captains in the league that upcoming games were going to be played without fans in the crowd. Italy by then had officially announced a countrywide lockdown, sparking concerns all over Spain. An hour later, our club announced the Friday game would indeed be played without fans in attendance. At the time, this sounded like the craziest thing ever. Later that same night, former President Trump announced a travel ban for non-U.S. citizens from Europe. At this point, every American player on my team began to understand how serious this virus was becoming. Basketball was quickly replaced in every player's mind by thoughts of family and safety.

I went from trying to prepare for the upcoming game to finding out the game had been officially canceled the next morning. By the afternoon, we were hearing entire regions of Spain would be going into lockdown. The next thing I knew, I was driving across the country to pick up my little sister, who was studying abroad in the south of Spain. After successfully retrieving her and driving back to my apartment, we stayed up all night trying to find plane tickets home. Luckily, we secured two.

Just a few days earlier, I was scheduled to play on Friday night. By that Friday afternoon, though, half of my teammates had joined me and my sister on planes out of the country in efforts to leave before lockdowns were put into effect. It all happened so quickly, so chaotically. Fortunately, we made it out and arrived safely back in the United States. At the time, that's all that mattered.

Fresh off the plane from Madrid, at the peak of global

uncertainty, we went straight into quarantine at our parents' house. China was seeing the worst at that point, followed by Italy and Spain. We felt like we'd barely made it out in time.

Home made things seem like there were two different worlds. Europe was a mess, and tensions there were through the roof. Once we arrived in the U.S., though, everything was relaxed. People didn't seem to worry about the virus at all. There was no testing; nobody had any idea how the virus was spread; everything was still open. There was so much unknown. This was bad news. We knew after what we'd experienced over the past couple days that it was only a matter of time before the States would be the new hot spot for the virus. Europe had already given us a grim forecast.

Coming home in this manner took a toll on me. I hadn't been home for nine months, and now my first encounter with my parents and sisters had to take place from the other side of a window. We waved through the glass and then pressed ourselves against it to give each other hugs. My dog, my best friend, cried outside my door for 14 days. He was confused about why I hadn't even given him a hug and couldn't hang with him after so much time had passed. His cries eventually turned into sadness, and he left my door, probably thinking that I'd forgotten him. It was heartbreaking.

We spent two weeks straight confined to the small side of our house filled with uncertainty. I'll never forget how weird it felt to be home after dreaming of returning during those tough, homesick times I'd had living so far away. I felt farther away from my family now than when I was on the other side of the world.

After two months in lockdown, the season was officially canceled. Since we were in first place when the season stopped, we were crowned league champions. It would have been nice to finish out the season and truly experience the benefits of a year's worth of hard work and sacrifice, but I was still thankful. Of course, it was a bummer that we couldn't celebrate the achievement together. A championship is still a championship, though, and it was special.

A year prior, I had ended my rookie season at the bottom of the league; now I was a champion. I had finally experienced a season of truly enjoying playing basketball. I had officially completed my goals. I was fulfilled.

I will forever be grateful for my experience in Valladolid.

AFTERWORD

"I cannot change the past, but I can help influence the future."
— C.S. Lewis

Coming off a championship at the pinnacle of my career, I had an extremely tough decision to make. The pandemic had made it a very tough time to be an athlete. Sports had been put on hold for months, and the idea of being only a professional athlete made me feel incredibly vulnerable. It was a wake-up call that basketball—like any sport—was truly just a game.

Eventually, discussions over a new season to be played amidst the COVID-19 pandemic began to take place. Those months during the peak of the pandemic were a time of brutal darkness, and playing the game of basketball was the least of my worries. All my focus was on making sure my family stayed safe, especially my grandparents who were at higher risk. Going to play the game I loved, when my family might suffer, felt selfish.

After long consideration, I decided to opt out of playing the 2020–21 & 2021-22 season. It was an extremely tough decision being at the peak of my basketball career, but it was ultimately the right decision. I had completed everything I had set out to accomplish.

I went from being a walk-on to scholarship player, then became a star player in college. I went on to become a professional basketball player who carried his team, and then became a strong member of a cohesive group that won a pro championship.

Most importantly, I discovered me.

"ME" = DELAYED GRATIFICATION x MICRO DISCIPLINE x CALCULATED MOMENTUM x INTENTIONALITY = "LIGHT,"

What else did I need to learn? It was time to apply "me" to the next endeavor.

If all else fails, I hope my story has provided you with a depiction of what the walk-on mentality truly is and how to apply it to any obstacle. The walk-on mindset can be brought to life no matter your position, status, or organization. Deep down it can be found inside each and every one of us.

Embrace the mindset. Embrace sacrificing for the longer goal. Embrace attacking the small details every day. Embrace doing more than what is asked. Embrace different fields. Embrace being an outlier. Embrace being multifaceted. Embrace intentionality. Embrace relentless curiosity.

Most importantly, don't let people box you in based on what they believe your identity needs to be.

Remember that within every situation there is always

a Light, at the End of the Bench—it's only a matter of discovering how to let your own Light, shine.

Always forward,
Niksha Federico

ENDNOTES

Aurelius, M. (2014). *Meditations* (M. Hammond, Trans.). Penguin Classics.

Clear, J. (2018). *Atomic Habits: tiny changes, remarkable results : an easy & proven way to build good habits & break bad ones.* New York, New York, Avery, an imprint of Penguin Random House.

Cultural Adjustment | Berkeley International Office. (n.d.). https://internationaloffice.berkeley.edu/living/cultural

Fogarty, L., & Kandler, A. (2020). The fundamentals of cultural adaptation: implications for human adaptation. *Scientific Reports*, *10*(1). https://doi.org/10.1038/s41598-020-70475-3

Manager, J. L. N. R. C. (2018, March 8). *The 5 most commonly asked questions about being a college walk-on.* USA TODAY High School Sports. https://usatodayhss.com/2017/the-5-most-commonly-asked-questions-about-being-a-college-walk-on

Rückel, L. (2019). Bench player versus line-up: the relationship between active playing time in team sports and mental… *ResearchGate.* https://www.researchgate.net/publication/330994690_Bench_player_versus_line-up_the_relationship_between_active_playing_time_in_team_sports_and_mental_well-being_competition_anxiety_and_satisfaction_with_the_coach

The Five Most Common College Walk-On Questions. (n.d.-a). SportsEngine. https://www.sportsengine.com/recruiting/five-most-common-college-walk-questions#:~:text=1.,financial%20aid%20(athletic%20scholarship)

ACKNOWLEDGEMENTS

I've been lucky to have the support of many wonderful people as this book has come together. I want to start out by extending my heartfelt thanks to my editor & advisor D. Bérnard. Your incredible talent and enlightened counsel improved the book in many ways. D.B's valuable insights, meticulous attention to detail, and overall enthusiasm were instrumental in refining the manuscript. I cannot emphasize how important he was in getting this project to the finish line. Something, I will forever be grateful for. To editor Travis Moran, for reading the manuscript with diligence and care, providing momentous structure and clarity throughout a crucial phase of the process. Travis thank you for always going above and beyond, it was a joy to work with you. Without Travis, I would have never known about the exceptional work of Dr. Oliver Eslinger. Thank you, Travis, for being a true professional.

I am thankful to my talented book designer Nuno Moreira, for having incredible patience and detailed commitment throughout. Nuno, thank you for your willingness to explore various concepts, and for your unwavering dedication to the project. Working with you on the cover design has been an absolute pleasure. To Sofia Marie Coronado, for the willingness to put her talented artistic touch on the project. Sofia, I had such a great time collaborating with you. Your phenomenal ability to turn words and ideas into visuals is something I am still in awe of. You are amazing. To JD Slajchert, for the unerring guidance, confidence, and charismatic optimism throughout the process of getting the book to completion. Your work-ethic and positive attitude towards the small things in life is something I admire and respect tremendously. Thank you for being you.

I will forever be indebted to Dr. Oliver Eslinger, for generously devoting both his time and valuable insight into the book. Doc, your contribution has been a game-changer for this project. Working with you has been inspiring, and I'll always remember our conversations over habits, systems, and performance on the Caltech campus. Doc you are a super star, and it is an honor to know you. Thank you, to many more.

A massive thank you to Mike Hansen for taking the time to write the Foreword. Mike I will forever be grateful for your willingness to contribute to the project. I remember when I first mentioned the prospect, there wasn't one ounce of hesitation. That meant a lot. Exchanging long voice messages back and forth towards completion is something I will always cherish. If you are reading this, I hope you know that I have the upmost respect for you. Looks like we have another thing to celebrate now. Lastly, to editor Barry Lyons, for the fine eye in proofreading. Thank you.

Several of the aforementioned read the manuscript at various stages, but particular thanks to Mikaela Kraus. Mikaela your notes, ideas, and thoughts were more valuable than you'll ever know.

I want to say thank you to all the coaches in my journey, whom I have been fortunate to learn so much from. To Coach Caceres, Holmes, & Cunningham, for showing me what it means to love the game, and the importance of community. To Coach Fisher & Dutcher, for teaching me the importance of patience, wisdom, doing little things right, and truly exemplifying everything the walk-on mentality stands for- having a vision and heart of a winner. To Coach V, for teaching me the art of discipline, the importance of being organized, and for taking a chance on me. To Coach Antonio Herrera, for teaching me the importance of handling adversity head on, and the inspirational power passionate work-ethic can have without even knowing. To Coach Hugo Lopez, for teaching me the art of charismatic leadership, the importance of winning every day, and what true respect feels like. Lastly, I want to thank Pepe Catalina, Mike Hansen, and the entire Valladolid organization, for seeing the potential in me, providing me with an opportunity, and bringing out the best version of myself both on and off the court – 'My gladiator forever'. To all my teammates who I have been fortunate enough to play with, root for, and win with. A brotherhood, a connection, and memories that I will hold close to my heart for a lifetime.

I am specifically grateful to Robbie Lemons, David Hollander, Dr. Oliver Eslinger, JD Slajchert, John Lohrenz, Lindsey Napela Berg, Kimbal Mackenzie, Hugo Lopez, Frank Bartley IV, Kingsley Okoroh, & D.B. Williams for generously devoting their time to support the project. Reading each of your kind words has truly been a humbling experience. Thank you.

Special thanks to Gerardo Martinez-Kuis, Hunter Moreno, Jacob Fujioka, Dj Viegas, Taylor, D'Erryl Williams, Parker U'u, Dakarai Allen, Kibret Woldemichael, Jonathan Briseno, Doug Marshall, Marco Johnson, Matt Soria, Mark Fisher, Dave Velasquez, Tim Shelton, Al Schaffer, Trent Suzuki, Emil Isovic, Darnell Bettis, and numerous other individuals I did not mention whose invaluable support have played a pivotal role in getting me here. You know who you are.

Lastly, to my family. I couldn't have done it without you guys. To my Mom, the day is finally here. I can't put into words how much you mean to me. You are the strongest person I know, the rock for so many. This book is for you, and I hope this is a small ounce to show how much I love you.

To my Dad. The most innovative man I know. Your creative approach to successfully push boundaries in science has been a great source of inspiration. Thank you for your constant support, and for motivating me to be better. Proud to be your son, love you.

Lastly, I would like to express my deepest appreciation to my beloved sisters: Tessya, Francesca, and Bella. Their enduring love and unwavering belief are treasures that I hold in the highest regard and for which I am immeasurably grateful. To Bella, you will always be the little one, but to see you grow into the strong woman you are is something I am most proud of. To Francesca, you amaze me every day. You are so graciously intelligent, and I will always be there for you. I love you more than you'll ever know. To Tessya, the journey of all journeys. Day 1 in every sense of the word, you are such a special person, and I am forever grateful to be your twin brother.

ABOUT THE AUTHOR

Niksha Federico's extraordinary journey from an anonymous 4-year Division 1 walk-on at San Diego State University, to a professional basketball player is nothing short of inspiring. Beyond the court, he is the founder of Ampl3, a non-profit organization dedicated to promoting sustainability in collegiate and professional basketball. With a diverse background spanning sports, technology, and philanthropy, Niksha continues to inspire positive change and innovative thinking. When not immersed in philanthropy, he mentors aspiring athletes, empowering the next generation to embrace a multi-faceted long-term mindset off the court. Born and raised in San Diego, CA, Niksha Federico's debut book, "Light, at the End of the Bench," encapsulates his story of grit and resilience redefining what it means to be a walk-on.

Email: lightattheendofthebench@gmail.com
Instagram: @nikshafederico
Ampl3: ampl3.org

www.ingramcontent.com/pod-product-compliance
Lightning Source LLC
Chambersburg PA
CBHW062104080426
42734CB00012B/2751